SIENA
SIX SUMMERS
OF MUSIC

SKETCHES OF AN AMERICAN PROGRAM
ABROAD

By James H. Semans, M.D.

Chairman, Board of Trustees,
North Carolina School of the Arts 1965—
Co-President, Siena Summer Session

(Edited by Eugene Rizzo and revised by the author)

Printed in the United States of America
by Meredith-Webb Printing Company of Burlington, North Carolina

Designed by John A. Furlow

Library of Congress Catalogue Card No. 73-81318

This publication
is dedicated to the memory of
Vittorio Giannini,
founding President of the
North Carolina School of the Arts

CONTENTS

ILLUSTRATIONS

PREFACE

The Siena Session of the North Carolina School of the Arts has proved so exhilarating that a survey of its development seems inevitable — just as the founding of the session itself seemed inevitable. The factors which gave birth to the project and have nurtured it all along have been destiny, musical talent, great hearts, and enough good judgment to meet and master each new challenge.

To understand the origins of the Siena Session, we must first look back to the Brevard Music Camp, located near Asheville, North Carolina. To this lovely mountainous region were attracted such artistic luminaries as the world-famous pianist, Gina Bachauer, and the Italo-American musicologist and composer, Vittorio Giannini.

The product of a musical family (his father was a famous tenor and his sister, Dusolina, a noted soprano), Vittorio Giannini had been dreaming since the early 1950s of founding an arts school where music, drama and the dance would be joined on a single campus. It was his conviction that these art forms are so interrelated that they could only benefit from physical proximity. He was thus years ahead of his time, for the cultural centers which sprang up all over the United States in the 1960s were squarely rooted in this same principle.

Giannini's dream eventually found a strong sponsor in Terry Sanford, Governor of North Carolina from 1961-65 and now president of Duke University. During Sanford's enlightened governorship, an advisory commission of artists approved the Giannini concept. A novelist named John Ehle, assistant to the Governor, turned a pragmatic pen toward writing a proposal to the Ford Foundation. The result was $5,000,000 from Ford and other foundations. Giannini thus had the financial backing to attract to North Carolina a faculty of eminence.

Even before the Ford grant was secured, Winston-Salem succeeded in raising $950,000 in an unprecedentedly swift two-day drive (40 percent from 2,000 Winston-Salem citizens and 60 percent from local private foundations), and the school was established in that city on a 22-acre tract which already included two school buildings.

At this point I was asked to accept a place on the board of trustees. A surgeon on the board of an arts school? My own musical background was that of an unsuccessful child violinist. Indeed, my memories of that dark period revolve around a keen and constant dissatisfaction with the results of contact between bow and strings. Nevertheless, persistence resulted in my traveling with the preparatory school orchestra — an accomplishment roughly equivalent to Sir Edmund Hillary conquering Mt. Everest. In any case, I was no born musician. That I became in later life a backer of the arts (or *appassionato*, as the Italians would put it) no doubt stems from my boundless admiration for those who can play beautiful music.

The North Carolina School of the Arts (for so Giannini's school would be called) held its first board meeting in July 1964 in the state capitol in Raleigh. Before the meeting, I was met outside by John Ehle, who confided that Governor Sanford planned to ask me to serve as chairman of the board of the new school. Already I had had doubts about participating on the board, and here I was being asked to head it! I hesitated and cautioned myself to "think it over."

My quandary was resolved by two other members of the board, Philip Hanes and Smith Bagley, both destined to become great friends. When these two eminent North Carolinians conspired to invite me for a beer and a chat, I asked them why they thought Governor Sanford wanted me as chairman of the board. To my astonishment, they told me it was because I was "interested in the arts." This certainly seemed an ironic statement, for Philip was about to become head of the Arts Councils of America, and Smith had run the Winston-Salem committee that in forty-eight hours had raised nearly a million dollars.

It was then that I began a real soul-searching about my interest in the arts. I discovered that beyond my experience as a violinist-appassionato, there existed an even deeper commitment to the idea of the arts. My surgical chief at Johns Hopkins, Hugh Hampton Young, with whom I had spent seven fruitful years, had shown me how exhilarating it could be to apply the "nothing-is-impossible" attitude of medicine to the fostering of projects in the arts. Himself a urological surgeon, he married into a musical family and somehow found time to raise funds for chamber music programs and for the Metropolitan Opera Company's annual visits to Baltimore. He was instrumental in the construction of the Baltimore Museum of Art and in the buying and renovating of Baltimore's Lyric Theater.

Doctor Young often packed as many as twelve of his residents and house staff into a theater box intended for eight. We would joyfully attend *Carmen, Tosca,* or *Faust* and then meet the divas and tenors at his home afterward. He even allowed a bit of gossip about himself and Lucrezia Bori in order to stir the bluestockings of Baltimore into supporting and attending the opera.

How to explain the charisma of this remarkable man? Suffice it to say that after being with Doctor Young for six or seven years, it took each of us residents at least half as much time again to "de-Young" ourselves and to resume our own personalities. But one was never quite himself again. We were instilled with a compulsion to give our full potential of service to society as well as to medicine.

Faced with this invitation from a brand-new school of the arts, I almost felt as though Doctor Young were beckoning to me from beyond the grave. Of course I would accept. And in so doing, I unwittingly cast my lot in the great artistic adventure that will occupy these pages.

ACKNOWLEDGEMENTS

A single telephone call from Rome to the governor's office in Raleigh made all the difference to the Siena Session. Without the approval of Governor Dan K. Moore — obtained through the request of his director of administration, Mr. Edward Rankin — these six summers abroad might never have taken place. This is the experience of faith which such a program needs.

The fact that so many people cared so deeply has generated a particular magic for the North Carolina School of the Arts Summer Session in Italy. I would like to extend my gratitude to these people for the part they played in this program.

To those innovators who, under the leadership of Governor Terry Sanford, initiated the North Carolina School of the Arts, and to the Legislature of North Carolina, which in its wisdom gave approval for the establishment of this institution, I offer my sincere thanks.

To Governor and Mrs. Moore, for their affirmative support of the school — scarcely a year old when Governor Moore took office — I extend gratitude coupled with a special word of thanks for their decision to make the Siena Session a tribute to the memory of Vittorio Giannini.

For their untiring efforts in opening the Session, scheduling it, arranging its myriad details and making the logistics work so brilliantly in the first years, I express deep appreciation to Giorgio and Adriana Ciompi, to Mary Ward and to Julia Mueller.

I am grateful in a special way for the inspired direction and guidance of the Foreign Minister of Italy, Amintore Fanfani, who dictated the charter of the Session and spelled out its curriculum. Vieri Traxler, now Italian Consul General in New York City, complemented this friendly act toward America by continuing his keen interest through the years as new plans were being devised for each new session.

We thank the music publisher Franco Colombo, friend and companion in exile of Amintore Fanfani during World War II, who first approached Fanfani with the idea of such a program. I single out for particular mention Danilo Verzili, President of the Monte dei Paschi di Siena, whose kindness and active support sustained us in many a difficult moment.

All these eminent Italians have continued a deep interest in the program since its inception.

We would also like to thank the Accademia Musicale Chigiana (two of our own faculty Giorgio Ciompi and Vartan Manoogian are among the distinguished faculty) for teaching the Master Classes and for their critical appraisal and warm approval of each year's performance at the Teatro Rinnuovati in Siena.

I am grateful for the concerned attention of Governor Robert W. Scott, who, like his predecessor Governor Moore, came to Italy to inspect the Session and inject his enthusiasm into the program, initiating a fund-raising project for its benefit at a crucial time. And I shall never forget the conscientious, stalwart friendship of Mr. R. B. Crawford of Winston-Salem who grappled with the difficult task of keeping Italian and American accounts during those first years.

Always, there has been the strength and ingenuity of President Robert Ward of the North Carolina School of the Arts.

There are indeed so many wonderful people who contributed to each element, each concert and each human relationship in these six summers that I am filled with the frustration of the inadequacy of words.

J. H. S.

THE FIRST STEPS IN FOUNDING THE SIENA SUMMER SESSION

In September 1966, one year after the opening of the North Carolina School of the Arts, my wife Mary and I were traveling through Switzerland on our way to Germany. The purpose of our journey was to observe the dormitory life of boys and girls in the Schule Schloss Salem in Baden, West Germany, an institution similar to the NCSA in that boys and girls of the same age group shared campus dormitory life together.

Before leaving Switzerland, we remembered that Vittorio Giannini, President of the NCSA, had said that something might develop in the way of a summer school in Italy for our music students. On a hunch, we called Vittorio in North Carolina. To our surprise, we learned that only an hour before he had received confirmation from the then Foreign Minister of Italy, Amintore Fanfani, that the school would become a reality the following summer. There were to be two meetings to plan the school: one on October 1 in Siena and another on October 5 in Rome. As chairman of the board of trustees of the North Carolina School of the Arts, I was asked to meet Vittorio in Rome and travel with him to Siena by car for the first of the two meetings.

I stayed in Rome at the Hotel Hassler. Typical of Vittorio, who seldom wasted words and never said anything until it became fait accompli, he left word that he would call me at the Hassler. But the message was never delivered, so I had to call all the way to North Carolina to find out where he was staying in Rome. Finally, I found him at the Grand Hotel. The following morning Vittorio, his New York publisher Franco Colombo, Consigliere Vieri Traxler (of the Italian Foreign Ministry, later Ministero Traxler, the Consul General in New York City) and I traveled together to Siena.

I had expected to hear about the school en route. Instead, we spoke about music and the Italian countryside. Finally, I realized that the purpose of this trip was simply for all of us to learn more about each other's personalities and experiences.

1

One interesting point in the conversation was brought up by Vittorio, who pointed out that the American pop singer was one of the few who enunciated his words well enough for the audience to understand them. He contrasted this with the Italian way of singing opera and the French treatment of the *chanson,* where attention to purely musical values often leads to the slurring of words.

When we arrived in Siena, there was some stirring in the region of the Palazzo del Capitano. This could only mean that Foreign Minister Fanfani was on his way, as all his local supporters were beginning to gather. With all the bustle in the sun-filled piazza — so reminiscent of a Renaissance painting — I was struck by how little, in certain ways, Italy has changed through the centuries.

We had a cup of espresso at a small bar and chatted until the foreign minister arrived. At this time, we gathered in a beautiful room on the second floor, the walls covered with pink silk and the ceilings delightfully frescoed. Everything was preserved much as it must have been in Medieval times. Movies were taken to document this meeting. Soon waiters — colorfully costumed and wearing white gloves — came in with trays of delicious aperitifs. It was all very festive.

Ceremony inaugurating the NCSA Summer Sessions. L-R: Giorgio Ciompi, Danilo Verzili, Foreign Minister Amintore Fanfani, Commissioner Padalino, myself and Mario Fabbri.

2

Foreign Minister Fanfani then dictated the rough draft of the school's charter and plans for the Summer Session, including everything from the round trip on Alitalia Airlines to the renting of pianos and students' tuition.

Following this meeting, a tour was made of the Palazzo del Capitano, the Accademia Musicale Chigiana, the Residenza Universitatis, the Hotel Continentale and the Villa Chigi* — the country house of the late Count Chigi, where Fanfani hoped eventually to establish permanently the Summer Session of the North Carolina School of the Arts. We also visited Pontignano, on the outskirts of Siena, where university students were living and it was thought our students might live and commute each day by bus. At a later date, a better plan was devised: all the students would be housed downtown in the somewhat old-fashioned Hotel Continentale, a five-minute walk to classes in the Chigiana.

Mary and I stayed over in Siena an extra day, but before leaving we attended a lush and beautiful banquet held at the Park Hotel (Villa Marzocchi). Speeches of expectation, enthusiasm and gratitude were exchanged between Foreign Minister Fanfani, Danilo Verzili (President of the Monte dei Paschi bank of Siena) and me. My speech had to be extremely extemporaneous and was translated skillfully by Traxler for the foreign minister and for those guests who did not speak English. I said that while our country's discoverer certainly had been Cristoforo Colombo, we had now been found by Franco Colombo, whom we also could not do without — inasmuch as he had been the one to bring us to Mr. Fanfani's attention. As Columbus had discovered America, so had Colombo discovered the North Carolina School of the Arts.

Mr. Fanfani answered this statement of gratitude on my part by saying that there were so many Italians in the United States that we did not even need the rare coincidence of two names for a happy relationship between America and Italy. The banquet was developing into a delight!

Among those present was Signora Bianca Fanfani (whose death two years later would be such a tragic blow to her husband), Signora Verzili (who sat beside me and spoke only Italian and French), the Minister of Cultural Affairs, Archi, and Commissioner Guido Padalino, the federal government's appointed Commissioner of Siena. The latter

---

*It was later taken over by a bank and converted into an electronic research center.

owed his office, I was told, to the fact that for two consecutive elections the Sienese had been unable to decide on a mayor.

The menu consisted of course after course of delicious food, the most unique of which were the tiny birds, or *uccellini*, no larger than one's thumb, which offered a single or perhaps two succulent bites of meat. We drank a very fine pink champagne* which had been named for Fanfani by a Spanish ambassador in gratitude for the former's having persuaded General DeGaulle to admit Spanish champagne into France. I must say that in addition to its sentimental significance and value, it was a delicious champagne.

* * * *

I cannot pass to other events without recording a significant agreement — expressed that day only verbally but faithfully adhered to — regarding the crucial first years of the Siena program. Seated between Traxler and Mr. Fanfani in the back of a Fiat, I was told by Fanfani that within five years he hoped we would be fiscally independent of the Italian government. Until that time, he said, he would recommend that the government help us. Of course, we could count on the moral endorsement of the Italian government forever.

Since that day, Mr. Fanfani has never failed to recognize me on sight or to initiate every encounter with a friendly "Va bene?" Nor have I, for my part, ever had cause to react with anything but complete satisfaction to the results of that first gala day.

The day after the banquet, Mary and I traveled back and forth to the places we had seen with Fanfani, checking routes and timing, etc. We were in a fever of excitement; the Siena program was becoming a reality. We left for Rome and the second meeting, set for October 5. On this occasion the charter was completed and another luncheon-banquet was held — this time in the beautiful marble dining room of the Farnesina (Foreign Ministry). The menus were specially printed for the occasion, and once again a superb wine was served.

We were now faced with the job of preparing our future students for a summer session in Italy. Vieri Traxler provided an Italian nobleman — the Marchese Uguccione Ranieri Bourbon del Monte di Sorbello — who gave two "orientation" sessions to answer the students' questions. But I am getting ahead of myself and will recount these happenings in their proper place.

---

*Champagne Fanfani, embottellado en el Castillo de Perelada, Costa/Brava, Prov. Gerana Espana.

SOME EARLY DIFFICULTIES

Following the Siena and Rome meetings, we returned to North Carolina to begin plans for an announcement ceremony which Fanfani was to have attended. Destiny, however, had other plans in store for us. Within a month of our return to the States, the November floods overwhelmed Florence, causing untold destruction and artistic loss. It goes without saying that the foreign minister was unable to visit North Carolina. Our own sense of confusion and loss was sharpened by the fact that Maestro Mario Fabbri, artistic director of the Accademia Musicale Chigiana, also headed the Cherubini Library — one of the buildings worst hit by flood waters.

Even more bitter a blow was the sudden death, a few weeks later, of Vittorio Giannini. I learned of this by long-distance telephone from Mary while I was in New York. Though Vittorio had suffered repeated heart attacks, his death was wholly unexpected and shocking to us all. Thus was the summer program deprived of its director even before the first session could begin.

Strangely enough — for the ways of fate are indeed unfathomable — we had already discussed Giannini's successor in Siena without realizing it at the time. During an informal supper in a restaurant in the Campo, Siena's famous square, the name Giorgio Ciompi had come up. Mary was speaking with Vieri Traxler, who related how he and his wife had lived for some time in Cleveland, where he had served as consul. It seems that Giorgio Ciompi, an extremely talented violinist, had helped Traxler organize an Italian affair in Cleveland shortly after Vieri's arrival there. His recollections of Ciompi were distinctly favorable. Giannini, also present at that supper, referred to Ciompi as an artist who knew his craft, a professional in the highest sense of the word.

Upon learning of Giannini's death, I asked Mary to call Vieri Traxler in Rome to see if Ciompi would be acceptable to the Italians as Giannini's successor. She did this, and within a few hours Traxler had checked both with the Chigiana and the Foreign Ministry. Ciompi's appointment was approved, and we were still in business for the summer of 1967.

The Florence floods had already struck by the time of Giannini's death, so we knew it would be impossible for Fanfani to attend the announcement ceremonies at the executive mansion in Raleigh. In his place came the Italian Ambassador to the United States, Sergio Fenoaltea, as well as Traxler and Danilo Verzili. We received excellent coverage in the press; to most Carolinians, the idea of a scholastic session in Siena rightfully seemed the source of great pride. Once again a luncheon banquet was held, this time with eloquent tributes in English to the memory of Vittorio Giannini and to the generosity of both the Italian government and the Banco Monte dei Paschi.

In brief, the program would make it possible for 120 gifted music students to travel to Italy for a 6-week period. Roundtrip transportation, room, board and sight-seeing expenses compared so favorably with that of other music camps that we were sure to attract students of the quality we desired.

And this is what we set out to do. Quite frantically Mary and I, together with Giorgio Ciompi and his charming wife Adriana, began to think of ways to bring the summer program to the attention of music students all around the United States. This was accomplished to some extent by the printing of two ads in the *New York Times*. Originally there was to have been only one ad, but since the first contained an unfortunate typographical error, we were granted a free second one.

Telephone calls, many of them long-distance, were made from teacher to teacher and teacher to student. That first year our musicians came from the Manhattan School of Music, Juilliard, the North Carolina School of the Arts, Curtis, Eastman, and Oberlin — as well as through the recommendations of various individual teachers on the West Coast. All in all, twenty-three states were represented. Incidentally, one of the students was the talented niece of Vittorio Giannini, Maura, around whom a small chamber group was built up.

The American faculty was made up of Olegna Fuschi and her husband, Howard Aibel; violinist Marc Gottlieb; the distinguished American soprano, Rose Bampton, and her accompanist, Herbert Horn. Giorgio Ciompi was artistic director.

At about this time, the Italians became concerned, even alarmed, by the amount of work they suddenly found on their hands. Not only were Ciompi and I in the States, fully 5,000 kilometers from Siena, but Mario Fabbri was still busy cleaning the mud off 10,000 sheets of ancient music in the Cherubini Library in Florence. It was not until the last day of January that Ciompi and I, Vieri Traxler, and Mario Fabbri got to sit down together in the Hotel Minerva in Florence to rough out what remained to be done.

Regularly every Saturday morning from February through June, Giorgio Ciompi and I would place a transatlantic call to keep abreast of events. Our main successes in that period were setting up a realistic class schedule for the Italian faculty and locating a hostelry in the outskirts of Rome, called the Domus Pacis, where ecclesiastic visitors to the Vatican often stayed.

A side trip to Siena in search of faculty lodgings proved largely unsuccessful. However, I did manage to reserve superb quarters in the Park Hotel for Miss Elizabeth Gotham so that she could watch the flowers grow from the air-conditioned sanctuary of her room. This unique lady, for many years "second parent" to our seven children, had survived no fewer than three fatal diagnoses in the span of fifteen years!

The outcome of the Florence meetings was extremely reassuring. Fabbri was given the opportunity to employ his general factotum, Franco Agostini, who moved from Trieste to Florence and later to Siena. Agostini, a talented pianist married to the sister of violinist Franco Gulli, had studied English at one time and was now faced with the task of relearning it. This required a great effort on his part, but he succeeded admirably and was invaluable in tackling and solving the many problems that first year occasioned.

MY FIRST PALIO

Shortly before the arrival of the students that summer, I attended the historic Palio in Siena. I had told them several months before in Siena that I intended to come, and arrangements were to have been made between the Accademia Chigiana and the head of the Tourist Board. However, when I arrived in Siena and called the Park Hotel to see if everything was in order, there was neither mail nor tickets for me. This pleased me, for I was suddenly free to go to the Palio like any other citizen in Italy.

Consequently I took off my tie and jacket and strode down to the Campo — where the Palio is held twice each summer — to inquire when the race would begin. I found the track closely surrounded by tables, parasols and thousands of people devouring ice cream and gulping down all manner of soft drinks. Within two hours there must have been 35,000 or 40,000 people packed into that one piazza! Ever since, I have thought of that crowd as being composed of standing and sitting sardines.

7

After the race, the winning contrada *holds a gala supper at which the honored guest is not the jockey (young man in light suit) but the horse!*

The bleachers for the immense crowd were placed in front of each shop. Not only did the shopkeepers have the right to sell the seats, but a narrow passageway was left open so that business went on as usual. And what an opportunity it was with 35,000 customers thirsting to be served.

Having purchased a ticket, I thought I could qualify as a sitting sardine. Alas, a small Sienese male, perhaps twelve years of age, soon talked me out of my seat so that his friend could sit next to him. All this was done in beautiful and slowly spoken, musical Italian — the best, I am told, in all of Italy. My ticket was challenged three times by one seller or another; had I not been able to refer to the owner of the shop who sold me mine, I am sure I would have stood up during the Palio even though I had paid a fancy figure for my seat.

The word "seat" in this case was a euphemism. In fact, I was wedged in like a Greek caryatid beneath a balcony so close to my head that I had to bend over during the entire Palio. Every now and then I stood up and chinned myself on the balcony in order to stretch my back. At one point, I espied a bit of bench that I thought I could lie down on if my back muscles cramped any more than they had already. I soon learned that this area was reserved for five waitresses who were frantically serving right up until the final moment. As soon as these valiant ladies were in place and the last three seats on the steps had been sold for a dizzying price, we were a solid mass of human beings ready for the race.

This was at about five or five-thirty. Then the procession began, lasting about an hour and a half. It was rather beautiful but slow and repetitive. Seventeen *contrade* — each representing an ancient quarter of the town — entered one after another, each with its own race horse and elected dignitaries. Medieval costumes, flag throwers, bands, drum rolls and the incessant tolling of Siena's great bell added up to a magnificent spectacle.

The sun, by now a flaming red ball, descended majestically behind Siena's famed gothic tower. Finally, the *Palio* itself — a silken banner with an embroidered figure of the Madonna — was borne in with great stateliness on an ox cart. By long tradition, the much coveted *Palio* is given to the *contrada* with the winning horse, whether or not the jockey is still aboard.

After such elaborate preparation, it surprised me that the race itself lasted less than three minutes. But what excitement! At least two horses were down with their riders thrown. The crowd made a deafening roar. Throughout the race, the riders beat their horses, each other's horses and even each other — all of which is allowed according to the ancient rules of the Palio. Never was there more genuine competition than in this horse race.

THE ARRIVAL OF THE STUDENTS

The excitement caused by the arrival of the students on July 10 was immeasurable. Driving out to Fiumicino Airport, I obtained special permission from customs to go out onto the airfield and film the moment of arrival. It was a great sight to see those students, most of whom had never before crossed the Atlantic. They told me that just before landing they had witnessed a magnificent Roman sunrise from 35,000 feet.

The four-day stay in Rome was crowded with events. Minister Fanfani insisted that the students see Rome and it set a wonderful tone for the whole program. Through the good offices of Senator Everett Jordan from North Carolina, we were all invited one evening to the residence of Ambassador and Mrs. Frederick Reinhardt.

9

The arrival on Italian soil, with Giorgio Ciompi (r.), soprano Rose Bampton and her husband, conductor Wilfrid Pelletier. In left background is Vieri Traxler, now Italian Consul General in New York.

The guest list was imposing; it seemed to include every person from Rome and the vicinity of Rome who was interested in the arts. Rose Bampton said that in all her long career as an artist she had never seen anything comparable done by an ambassador. At sundown, torches were lit in the garden, and a beautiful buffet supper was served. Fanfani and Traxler attended this event, and both greeted the students eagerly.

On another occasion the foreign minister, a very versatile and busy man, arranged to meet with our students at the Ministry right after he had finished teaching his morning economics class at the University of Rome. Before being served a delicious buffet lunch, we were led into a beautiful room with high ceilings and treated to a brief lecture by the Marchese di Sorbello. The Marchese advised the students to construct small dictionaries for their own use, to read the Italian newspapers and to avoid discussions about Viet Nam!

Thus a crowded week came to a close. There were televised news interviews with Minister Fanfani present, and this created great publicity not only in the Roman papers but in the important *Nazione* of Florence. The students were taken by bus to Orvieto and then on to Siena. I went to swim in Rome's olympic pool, but would rather have slept twelve hours to recover from the rigors of that first week.

10

I don't want to go any further with my narration without including a description of the two institutions in Siena whose intimate cooperation has been essential to the life of the program: the Monte dei Paschi di Siena and the Accademia Musicale Chigiana. If the "Monte" as a bank has several unique features, the same can be said for the Chigiana as a musical conservatory. The former is absolutely atypical as a banking institution in the extent to which it has selflessly served public interest for five centuries. The latter, though founded as a conservatory by the last Count Chigi in 1932, has always functioned less as a conservatory than as a "gathering of artistic energies."

But I don't wish to steal a march on the two descriptions that follow. First of all, let's have the bank. No one better sketched in for an American audience the importance of the Monte dei Paschi di Siena than Vieri Traxler, Consul General of Italy. The occasion was a speech delivered at the International Banking Convention held in 1970 in Chapel Hill, North Carolina. With Vieri's permission, I am including here an adaptation of that address.

THE MONTE
DEI PASCHI DI SIENA

After all the excellent speeches we've been regaled with today, some of you will look upon this speech of mine rather the way one looks at rice at the end of an enormous Chinese dinner — that is, with no appetite whatever.

The Monte dei Paschi di Siena is a bank and not a minor one. As far as size is concerned, it is in fact the seventh bank in Italy and about the sixtieth in the world. It has offices and branches all over Italy and some offices in foreign countries. It is not its size which makes it noteworthy but some of its characteristics. These include its name and age, its peculiar nature, and the use it makes of its profits. Its age is remarkable. Even though the Monte dei Paschi was chartered as recently as 1625, it nevertheless incorporated another institution which had been in existence since 1472. Consequently, the bank predates the discovery of America by some two decades.

11

Former Governor Terry Sanford (instrumental in founding the NCSA) and his wife Margaret Rose visited the Session in Siena during the summer of 1971, the year in which he became president of Duke University.

The second noteworthy thing is the name. Monte dei Paschi literally means "mountain of pastures," which gives it a kind of Oriental flavor but was in fact at the time of its founding an extremely accurate and technical description of what the bank was. The word *monte* in Italian (literally "mountain") was used in the Middle Ages to describe any pooling together of financial resources for a specific purpose. Thus we have still in Italy and in France a number of very worthwhile institutions — in effect, state-owned pawnbrokers which lend money to people against the deposit of some object. They are called *monti di pietà* (literally "mountains of compassion") because they were created — the one in Siena in 1472 — for the specific purpose of giving credit to needy people at a reasonable interest.

Unlike private pawnbrokers, these institutions are in business not to make money but to provide a service. Because they can make loans with very reasonable interest rates, they are the mainstay of many citizens who experience frequent financial ups and downs — such as students, for instance. I myself used to be a faithful customer of the mountain of compassion in Florence in my student days.

The word *monte*, as I said, was used to describe an accumulation of financial resources for a specific purpose. In the year 1625 the econ-

12

Governor Dan Moore, Sanford's successor in Raleigh, strolling with Doctor Semans down Siena's main street on an inspection tour during our second session abroad.

omy of the city of Siena needed a shot in the arm. The city had just recently become part of the Granddukedom of Tuscany after a very cruel war, and its financial resources were somewhat paltry. So the city fathers pleaded with the Grand Duke of Tuscany to be allowed to set up a bank that could give credit to local tradesmen, artisans and farmers. The grand duke agreed to this and also provided the means with which to start the bank. His solution was, for those days, extremely modern and quite brilliant.

For centuries the city of Siena had owned a lot of rich grazing land — pastures which were located partly near the city and partly near the mountains of Maremma. The city derived a sizeable income from these pastures by exacting a fee from the cattle owners who wanted to send their herds to feed there. These pastures, together with the conquest of the city by the grand duke, had become part of the crown lands. So the grand duke selected an area of these pastures, valued it at 200,000 ducats, and pledged it to the new bank.

Note that he didn't give it but pledged it as collateral to be used if the bank should be liquidated. Together with the capital he gave also the rental — valued at 10,000 ducats or 5 percent of the capital. Now, armed with these resources the bank immediately issued 2,000 bonds

A rare meeting of church, state and science: Mary Semans chats with (l-r) Siena's Mayor Roberto Barzanti; His Eminence Mario Castellani, Archbishop of Siena; Doctor Albert Sabin, developer of the oral polio vaccine; and visiting Governor Bob Scott of North Carolina.

at 100 ducats each and sold them to the public. Since these bonds were guaranteed by the pastures and carried 5 percent interest, they sold like hot cakes, and the bank was soon in business with 200,000 ducats working capital.

Since the origin of this money came from these grazing lands or pastures, the bank was given the name "mountain of pastures" — and the name hasn't changed nor has the bank. From the beginning it was a public institution owned by the city of Siena and by the state of Tuscany and designed primarily to support the economy of the city of Siena. Its directors are appointed in part by the Italian government and in part by the city government in Siena. All of its resources, or rather net profits, are divided in two parts: 50 percent goes — as it went in the past — to increase the working capital of the bank, and the other 50 percent (and this is one of the interesting features) has to be spent for the benefit of the city. It <u>has</u> to go into the city.

14

Therefore, to give you just a few examples, in the last few years the bank has paid for a new street lighting system in the city of Siena, it has built highways to improve the communications of the city, it has financed the construction of new hospitals, and has given to the University of Siena a whole new department of banking sciences — the first of its kind in Italy and one of the few existing in the world.

But equally noteworthy has been the role that the bank has played in supporting the arts. This is understandable for two reasons, the first of which is that Siena has an ancient tradition of artistic expression. Together with nearby Florence, the city can be said to have co-founded the Renaissance — at least in the area of figure painting. The other reason can be explained by something in the Italian national character, something which would seem to disagree entirely with the state motto of North Carolina, which says "It is better to be than to appear." I would say that in Italy the contrary might be said: "If you don't look good, you are a nobody." It is normal for any self-respecting institution in Italy to devote a certain amount of money to appearances; in the case of the Monte dei Paschi, this took the form of commissioning beautiful art works. As early as 1481, a painter and sculptor from Siena received such a commission from the bank. Their works of art are still in the bank today.

One recent example of this munificence toward the arts by the bank has been its support of the well-known music institution which is the Accademia Chigiana. It is exactly in this role of patron of the arts that this bank in this city in the middle of the hills in Italy came to play a minor but not insignificant role in the life of the state of North Carolina. As you have heard, Vittorio Giannini, the first president of the North Carolina School of the Arts had a project — or rather, a dream — that he wanted to take some of the outstanding music students from this country to Italy to expose them to Italy's musical life and culture and thus enrich their education. Our then foreign minister, Amintore Fanfani, learned of this project, and he immediately thought it appropriate that such a program take place in Siena; he knew that in Siena there was this institution, this bank which had the funds and the ability to use them for the purposes discussed. After negotiations the program was started and, as you know, has been extremely successful.

To my mind, this particular program is one of the more intelligent examples of international cooperation in the field of cultural exchange. It is not odd that such a relationship should spring up between a school in North Carolina and a bank in Siena. The state of North Carolina has a name and reputation and a unique tradition in the field of education. It is particularly gratifying that this vision could have been matched by Minister Fanfani and by this old "mountain of pastures", which has proved once more that an old institution can find new ways to express itself and to contribute to the world of today.

Governor Bob Scott (r) and his wife Jessie Rae (c) plunging eagerly into a student reception after one of our orchestral concerts.

16

Severino Gazzelloni, Italy's "golden flute," giving a master class in one of the frescoed rooms of the Chigiana.

THE CHIGIANA
A UNIQUE INSTITUTION

The raison d'être of the North Carolina Summer Session in Siena was best defined in the charter dictated personally by Amintore Fanfani, then foreign minister, at the first meeting between the two organizations on October 1, 1966 in the Accademia Chigiana itself:

> The courses instituted by the North Carolina School of the Arts will not interfere with the activity and the character of the Accademia Chigiana, which will remain unchanged. The Chigiana will continue to offer postgraduate courses for the perfection of solo instruments. For the organization and realization of the Carolina courses a new institution will be created, directed, and administered jointly by the North Carolina School

17

of the Arts and the Accademia Musicale Chigiana. Courses of eight weeks in length will be given by American teachers brought by the North Carolina School of the Arts and by Italian teachers of high professional level recommended by the Accademia Chigiana. Lectures, concerts, demonstrations by eminent artists, foreign and Italian, will be organized by the Accademia and integrated into these courses. Students attending the summer session will also attend all manifestations of the Accademia Chigiana to complement their own regular courses.

One can detect, even in the legal diction employed by Minister Fanfani, something of the unique character of the Chigiana and the emotions it generates. How careful he is to insure its immutability, to delimit the frontiers between the two instituions.

One can sense the special quality of the Chigiana simply by seeing it. A gothic palace dating in large part from the twelfth century, it would have earned its place as a major tourist attraction even without its rich musical associations. Its halls are hung with paintings by Beccafumi, Sodoma and Botticelli; tapestries, mosaics, baroque clocks, gilded mirrors, frescoed ceilings and Renaissance chests vie with one another for the eye's attention. To step inside its giant portals is to be uplifted by art.

In this noble setting flourished the Chigi-Saracini, an ancient family that over the centuries produced two popes, a handful of cardinals and a long line of affluent bankers. It is a happy accident for the future of the Muses that the last member of this noble line — the Count Guido Chigi-Saracini, who lived alone with a staff of some thirty servants — was an ardent music-lover who left everything he owned for the purpose of fostering musical excellence.

There are many stories about the Count and his eccentricities (Winthrop Sargeant wrote an excellent profile in the September 3, 1960 issue of *The New Yorker*), but the one I like most concerns his musical conservativism. Enthusiast that he was, the Count simply drew the line after Brahms. The suggestion of Stravinsky risked scowls, and anything more modern — heaven forbid! — was a courtship with apoplexy.

On one occasion, the famed Budapest String Quartet was invited to give a recital in the hallowed halls. After a perfectly traditional program — something along the lines of Haydn, Schubert, and Mendelssohn — the musicians were induced, by what is always referred to in the papers as "deafening" applause, to do an encore. Either unaware

18

or momentarily forgetful of the Count's musical predilections, the four men innocently set about playing a movement from a Bartok quartet.

Fortunately for those in the audience, the Count habitually sat not among the general public but with a few special guests in a small, exquisite room to the right of the stage. The Hungarians hadn't got too far along before the Count, stricken with horror, raised himself and advanced unsteadily toward the wings. Brandishing a walking stick, the last of the Chigis shammed shut an immense mirrored door with what must have sounded like a thunder clap from the Last Judgment.

Though this story presents the Count in a somewhat equivocal light, he was actually one of art's great "angels" — as they say on Broadway. A lifelong friend of composer-librettist Arrigo Boito, he played a critical role in the worldwide revival of interest in the music of Antonio Vivaldi. Upon his death in 1965, he left everything — palace, paintings, extensive landholdings — in trust with the Monte dei Paschi for the perpetuation of a musical ideal.

In its own way, this "ideal" has proven to be as unique as the building that hosts it. Every summer, a number of the world's most distinguished performer-teachers — Chigiana regulars have included Alfred Cortot, Andres Segovia, Franco Ferrara, Severino Gazzelloni — gather in its frescoed rooms to conduct master classes. What is interesting about the administrative structure of the Chigiana is that there seems to be a tacit understanding among faculty members and all others concerned to keep it as decentralized as possible. The single goal of everyone is to attain musical excellence in a climate as free as possible. To a surprising extent, mutual respect has replaced hierarchy.

As Fanfani dictated in the charter, the Chigiana courses differ from the Carolina courses in that they are on a postgraduate level and entirely devoted to development of solo playing. Our courses, conducted a month earlier by a combined American and Italian faculty, involve younger students (from sixteen to twenty-two years of age) destined, in most cases, for orchestral playing.

I think I can say that one of the more interesting features of the Carolina-Chigiana association is that it has been different in each of the six sessions. We have run the gamut from total integration (the year our student orchestra played in the Settimana Senese — the Chigiana's annual festival) to a mere tenant-landlord status. But never has the relationship failed to be beneficial to both sides, and I'd like to say something about that.

Two great teacher-performers: violinist Franco Gulli (l) and cellist Janos Starker (r) talk things over between classes in the courtyard of the Chigiana.

The single fact of exposure to, and instruction by, foreign musicians has been of inestimable value to our young instrumentalists. For them, music as a universal language was no mere cliché but a classroom reality. It is an inspiring thing to witness — as I have — a student making a real breakthrough in the mastery of his instrument under the guidance of a man who speaks not a word of English!

To be sure, some of our Italian professors (Gulli is one) have been fluent in English; violinist Brengola, I recall, spoke French in class because two of our young Americans were more or less proficient in that tongue. But in the majority of cases (Gazzelloni is an example), the professors have expressed themselves in a charming patois of two languages, mingling Italian words of encouragement (*"Bello, molto bello"*) with stern if quaint English commands (*"*You stop!*"*).

In some cases, our students were so enriched by the experience that they elected to stay on after the Carolina session to enroll, pending acceptance, in the Chigiana master classes. This has happened very often over the years, even in the case of the fabled conducting classes offered by Franco Ferrara, said to be the heir of Toscanini.

Often enough, the helping hand has been so direct as to pass almost unnoticed. A case in point would be Gulli's recommendation the pre-

Post-concert exhilaration is written on the faces of (l-r) John Kennedy, Sandra Miller and Phil Wachowski after a 1969 performance at the Chigiana.

vious year that our first violinist join a summer junket with a Swiss chamber group. While the NCSA orchestra was en route to Rome for their final concert of the session, Mr. Joseph Genualdi, age twenty, was boarding a jet that would take him to Lucerne and his first professional assignment.

And what, you may ask, have we brought to the Chigiana in return? First of all, boundless enthusiasm, typically American, that has rarely failed to impress our hosts. Some of our students (their faces flash through my mind as I write these lines) took to the experience so strongly that they ran with indiscriminate enthusiasm from private lessons to orchestral rehearsals and on to examine the frescoes in Siena's duomo. This type of response can only be infectious; it helped the Italians to see their old world with new eyes, and on more than one occasion, they communicated their gratitude for this.

On a more tangible level, we brought them an orchestra. It may surprise many Americans to know that one of the striking facets of our culture is a super abundance of well-trained and coordinated orchestras.

21

Gene Rizzo (l) leading one of his many walking tours – this one to Siena's art gallery (Chigiana in background).

Perhaps it is significant, even symbolic, that the courses at the Chigiana are aimed at the development of virtuosi while those of the NCSA point to ensemble playing. The high marks of Italian culture have always been the triumphs of individual creativity. Think of such rebel-geniuses as Da Vinci, Michelangelo, Galileo. In America, a country of barely 200 years, our most splendid chapters have always been the product of collective efforts — rarely of individual genius. I think of President Kennedy's witticism the night he offered a dinner for our Nobel Prize winners at the White House. "Gentlemen," he is reported to have said, "there hasn't been so much intelligence gathered in this room since the last time Thomas Jefferson dined here alone."

However one analyzes the dynamism of different cultures, there is no doubt that our NCSA orchestras have always made an impact in Italy. Students though they were, the integrated sound they produced with the opening measures of a Beethoven or Dvorak symphony never failed to hold the complete attention of our listeners. I recall one Italian, frankly stunned by the warmth of the orchestral sound at a concert we gave in the beautiful romanesque abbey of San Lucchese, not far from Siena. "*Non sono studenti,*" he exclaimed with admiration, "*sono stupendi!*"

22

Two of our soloists in the 1972 session: mezzosoprano Donna Stephenson (l) and soprano Beverly Culbreath (r), North Carolinians both.

CIOMPI RUNS INTERFERENCE

One time Giorgio Ciompi and I stopped at the Continentale on our way to a concert and noticed a soldier skulking near the desk. Giorgio, being a Florentine and consequently quick to size up any situation, immediately asked the soldier his reason for being there. The young man responded that he had a girl's room number and wanted to go up and see her. Giorgio, who felt a real paternal responsibility toward the students, went to the elevator and gave the girl in the room a sermon instead of the "serenade" that her soldier boyfriend had intended.

MATTERS OF THE HEART

No one would be surprised to hear that there were cases of romance in a program that involved 120 students ranging in age from 16 to 22. As Giorgio Ciompi said, "At that age one either loves or hates someone or something," so that each year there had to be some advice given to temper infatuations and to save the parties concerned from some disaster of the heart.

Indeed, on one memorable occasion the artistic director was routed from bed at three o'clock in the morning with the demand that a rabbi be found to marry two instrumentalists. Since rabbis are hard to come by in Siena (not to mention at three in the morning), it was agreed that it might be postponed until the morning — and in the morning the request was not repeated!

In another instance, a sixteen-year-old musician appeared in a state of great anxiety saying that he had been invited to dinner at the home of an Italian family whose daughter he had been dating. He was extremely apprehensive over the news of the Italian tradition — still in force to some extent — that such invitations often reflect the seriousness of the relationship. First the delicate question of any deep commitment on his part had to be settled. It was with great relief that he learned that if indeed there was no family in the offing, his obligations were no greater than those he might feel in his own country.

A PALIO FOR APOLLO 8

Soon after the splashdown following the first lunar landing by the Americans, we were seated at luncheon in Siena as the guests of Danilo Verzili. The occasion was the launching, not of an Italian space program, but of that year's master classes at the Chigiana. Various dignitaries were invited, and we were all feeling the elation that follows good food, wine, speechmaking and vociferous handclapping.

At the height of festivities, Avv. Verzili — my co-president for the Siena summer session — turned to me in front of everyone and said: "Semans, if you bring us the astronauts, we'll have a special Palio in their honor!" Now this would have been special indeed, for the dates of the Palio are inalterably fixed at July 2 and August 16. Only once in a blue moon (or "once every Pope's death" as the Italians say) is there ever a third Palio — though it has been known to happen.

I tried to picture myself as a man of influence sufficient to convince NASA to include Siena and the Palio on the next tour of the astronauts. It was not inconceivable — the astronauts after all did travel throughout the Western world. But this is how it happened: The following summer, Mary and I traveled to Venice in the company of the Traxlers. There we visited the Lido and had the good luck to witness the Festa del Redentore, the annual celebrations that com-

24

With astronaut James Lovell and his children in the board room of the Monte dei Paschi di Siena

memorate the end of the plague in that city. It was a stirring sight: dozens of brightly colored barges floating about the Grand Canal, surrounded by gondolas, vaporetti and countless little boats filled with merrymakers.

Our holiday atmosphere dissolved upon our return to Siena in time for the Palio. A series of crises — at the rate of one or two a day — combined to lower my spirits by degrees. I began to hope for one of those frequent acts of fate that have ever enlivened our summer program abroad. As it turned out, I didn't have long to wait.

That same afternoon, just as I was returning to our rooms at the Park Hotel, I found the telephone ringing with what seemed like more than usual insistence. I picked it up and found it was one of Danilo's lieutenants, shrilling "Astronauti! Astronauti!" in an excited voice. I couldn't conceive of what had happened. Finally a familiar name came through — "Lovell! Lovell!" — and I remembered that James Lovell was indeed one of the astronauts who had journeyed into space on the Apollo 8 expedition the year before.

The message was that we were urgently requested to come to the board room of the Monte dei Paschi bank, where Lovell was being entertained with his wife, daughter and son. Mary and I hastened to this command performance, delighted that at last destiny had dealt us another ace. I became so exhilarated that I even allowed myself for a moment or so to believe that the Italians might possibly assume that it was I who had brought the astronaut to Siena.

Lovell seemed to enjoy tremendously the spectacle of the Palio. I believe he also enjoyed hearing at long last the American version of the English language. He had an Italian bilingual interpreter, but this probably wasn't half so homey as a North Carolina accent. His wife was from Michigan; together they cut a real *bella figura* for America. His restraint and modesty, I am sure, were pleasing to the Italians. Not a single word was said about the one subject I'm sure was at the back of everyone's mind — namely, we were in the presence of a man who had seen the moon, not in his fancy, not as an emblem of romance, but as a physical reality!

MY MUTE COMPANION

On one of my many ship-crossings on the way to Siena, I had a great opportunity to practice my Italian. The system that I followed was to study the conversational Italian phrasebooks very carefully in my cabin before emerging and "trying it out" on the great variety of staff members that comprised the ship's crew. I felt that since I was their guest they would feel the obligation to tolerate my Italian up to a point. In fact, they might even help me with it, which indeed they did most enthusiastically.

Consequently, every venture from my stateroom was for me an Italian "lesson." In the dining salon, I would study all the items on the menu rather than pass it back to the waiter as soon as I had ordered. Not only did this improve my grasp of Italian, but it protected me from overeating. With each passing day, the waiter became less a waiter and more a *professore* correcting my pronunciation. I would even memorize jokes out of my phrasebook in an attempt to distract him from forcing too much food on me.

On this same voyage, there was a passenger who had had brain surgery in New York and was convalescing on his way back to Europe.

The Piazza del Campo and the Palazzo Pubblico: scene of many lively discussions between students and faculty.

His presence was mildly upsetting to a number of the passengers, owing to the fact that he could not speak. Indeed, it was never clear how much he understood of what others said. Even if he had been able to speak, it would have been in Greek, a language hopelessly obscure to most of the people on board. However, he was able to make it clear that he would like to purchase a suit of clothes when we arrived at Naples. I took this on as a project, and vowed then and there that I would use my limited Italian not only to purchase a good suit of clothes for him but at a good price. Since we'd have more than enough time to purchase the suit, I thought that we might also see some theater.

Upon our arrival in Naples, we disembarked and plunged into the busy life of the city. As we rode by what turned out later to be the San Carlo Opera (at that time unfamilar to me), I noticed a poster curled about a column. I could only read the two words "Un Ballo" — which I knew in English meant "dance". Perfect! Here was a "language" common even to my patient passenger friend — whom I was determined to see entertained. In great haste, we stopped the taxi and purchased two tickets. Then came the revelation: I had not read all the way around the pillar; the spectacle was not a dance but a performance of the Verdi opera *Un Ballo in Maschera* ("The Masked Ball").

My initial disappointment was soon overcome by the sheer beauty of the music. Since our "dance" tickets were for the first row, we could see and hear everything to perfection. Not only was it my first visit to the famous San Carlo, I believe it was the first time I heard an Italian audience hiss a singer. I'm not sure whether this was because he was a foreigner or just a weak singer, but I am inclined to the latter view. Even I could hear that he was a little flat on several of the high notes.

We proceeded from the opera to the clothing store. Forced to speak, I discovered how remarkably improved my Italian was. I wanted to protect my colleague from paying too high a price or from choosing the wrong material. To judge by what our fellow passengers said subsequently, I must say that we came off very well. Incidentally, I can recommend this "baptism by fire" method of language learning as an excellent means of acquiring relative fluency in short order.

THE SOUND OF MUSIC

The Palazzo del Capitano, only a few steps from the duomo, was a beehive of activity that first year. Not only did Rose Bampton hold her vocal classes there, but it was the meeting place for the piano courses conducted by Olegna Fuschi and her husband Howard Aibel.

Who could have counted the pianos in that building? The energetic team of Fuschi and Aibel had set things up in such a way that each of their twenty-six students could practice six hours every day. This created a panic situation for the general factotum, Sig. Agostini, who seemed to spend every minute ordering pianos from Milan and surrounding areas. No one had found the time to use a pencil and paper before the session to find out exactly how many pianos would be necessary for each student to practice six hours a day — exclusive of siesta time, of course.

The question of the siesta was a thorny one. In the mind of the Italian, the siesta is a sacred and inviolable period of the day. In those early afternoon hours, no noise, no invasion of his peace and quiet will be tolerated. At the same time, one can easily imagine all the

"One can easily imagine all the scales that came wafting out of that building."

scales — vocal and pianistic — that came wafting out of that building. Quite literally, tomatoes would come sailing through the open windows of the palazzo whenever too many decibels emanated at the wrong hour of the day.

Indeed, there was even a hastily convoked meeting of the city fathers to decide what to do about these "invaders" from North Carolina who simply did not understand the importance of the siesta. On another occasion, we had to rustle up another lodger for a landlady who claimed that our musicmaking had driven away the previous one. We settled this by finding her a real live music lover.

In general, the Italians are very tolerant of music — even when it's still in the rehearsal phase. This made us feel very good as visitors in Siena. The situation, however, was not without its ironic moments. I recall one American family strolling up Siena's main street and past the Hotel Continentale. They could not have known that its denizens were fellow Americans. Hearing the sweet din from within, one of them was heard to say, "You see, Dad, I told you you'd hear music in the streets in Italy."

29

NOSTALGIA

Surprisingly few cases of homesickness have been verified through the years in Siena. I say "surprisingly" because a large number of the students had never before been out of North Carolina, not to mention the United States.

In general, we have learned that although it has been a great advantage and simplification to have all of our students living in one hotel, it has tended to inhibit their interest in learning Italian. A great dream of our is to see the students housed with Italian families — either individually or in pairs — where they would certainly learn Italian. So far, the language courses we have arranged have never been well attended, not even when they were in conjunction with preparatory courses given before leaving the United States.

A REMARKABLE MAN

Shortly after meeting my Italian colleague, Danilo Verzili, I learned that he was not only the head of the Monte dei Paschi di Siena (founded 1472) but was also president of the Banco Toscano, in addition to having several other business responsibilities in Rome. I knew then that I would come to understand this man only by observation and gradual involvement with him.

Since my philosophy of life as a doctor is to like everybody (who can imagine a doctor who dislikes a patient), it was in this spirit that I set about understanding the man and his functions. Our meetings were always in a climate of amusement, good friendship, candor — never confrontation. The dominant mood was a shared desire to express personal as well as international friendship.

What amused me at first was the silent estimate I could see Verzili making of me, his American co-president, as he moved the centerpiece of flowers that made us invisible to each other and pressed me with as much wine and delicious food as he possibly could. I recall staving off his repeated offers of more wine by keeping my wine glass, with the constant addition of water, always at brim level. Indeed, conviviality characterized every luncheon or dinner that we ever had together.

Co-Presidents of the NCSA Summer Sessions, bank president Danilo Verzili and James H. Semans, M.D.

We always needed an interpreter. I even acquired a gadget which served as an extension from the telephone receiver to the ear of an interpreter so that our telephone calls would not go awry. This device served us well on more than one occasion.

Verzili's industry and acumen have kept him at the helm of the Monte dei Paschi Bank for three terms of four years each — the longest in the bank's history of 500 years! The man has unbounded energy, a fact expressed even by his physical presence. It seems that Danilo's intensity has honed his body to something lightweight and ultra-practical.

Just keeping up with him is a job in itself. Three days he is in Siena, the other four in Rome, and then there are the countless mad dashes between the two cities in his chauffeur-driven car. These famous jaunts, clocked at two hours flat on the Highway of the Sun,

31

find Danilo either catnapping in the back seat or reading all the Italian newspapers.

Danilo is complemented by his charming and beautiful wife, Teresa, who supplies all the relaxation and composure that one might not otherwise feel in dealing with her busy husband. He loves an intense exchange of ideas. If one is resourceful, Danilo appreciates the energy per se that goes into the support of a controversial attitude, even one he bitterly opposes. Above all, he has qualities of loyalty to a cause, loyalty to other people, a signal courageousness that make him a remarkable man.

PUTTING ON A CONCERT

I don't think it is possible or desirable to conclude these sketches without saying something more specific about our concerts abroad. Of the three dozen or so orchestral concerts that the North Carolina School of the Arts has put on in six summer sessions, I should like to select one that will illustrate some of the extreme exhilaration that these events regularly generate.

I will talk about the concert in the Campidoglio with which we concluded the 1970 summer session. This is a beautiful piazza, the site of the Capitol, and said to be the spot where Romulus and Remus founded the city of Rome. Legend or not, there are ample Roman ruins beneath the piazza, so we know the place was already antique when Michelangelo set about redesigning it in the third decade of the sixteenth century. The result is one of the most harmonious, eye-pleasing piazzas in all of Italy; and when it is illuminated at night, it is almost unbearably beautiful. Not surprisingly, Sophia Loren has an apartment overlooking this jewel-box square.

The idea of our giving a concert there grew out of an exchange of letters between Robert Ward, President of the North Carolina School of the Arts, and Mr. Frank Wigglesworth, then director of the American Academy in Rome. Fortunately for us, the succeeding director, Bartlett Hayes, picked up the correspondence when he came into office and showed great interest in implementing and sponsoring the project.

In Rome, I joined forces with Bartlett Hayes of the American Academy in approaching our Italian colleagues. We were received

These post-concert bouquets for Nelsie Walker, a Juilliard student and soprano soloist in our 1971 session, anticipated by a year her winning the important Jenny Lind Award.

most warmly by one of the mayor's deputies, Sig. Mario Mazzocchi, in charge of all visiting delegations and ceremonies pertaining to local government. Together, we discussed such problems as blocking off traffic during the concert, turning off the large fountain in the Piazza Campidoglio, putting in seats for the audience, and insuring sufficient illumination for the musicians to read their scores.

I learned at this time that the mayor of Rome might not be able to attend. We were told that if this were the case, we would not be able to invite Mr. Fanfani either, for Italian protocol dictates that there should be no one present who outranks the mayor if the mayor himself is not on hand to show hospitality. This turned out to be a moot question, as Fanfani — who had recently been named president of the Italian Senate — had to preside over an evening session on the day of our concert.

Instead, the performance was attended by the deputies both of Mayor Darida and President Fanfani; also there were Danilo Verzili, President of the Monte dei Paschi di Siena, and United States Ambassador to Italy, Graham Martin. By happy coincidence the ambassador was a North Carolinian, so he followed the event with more than usual attention and pride.

Meanwhile, preparations for the concert proceeded at a frantic pace. We had recently engaged the services of a young American publicist-journalist resident in Italy, and he set about designing and printing a program, commissioning a tasteful and eye-catching poster, and gathering as many press contacts as possible. His crowning achievement was arranging an article (with photo) by Alfred Friendly, Rome correspondent for the *New York Times* — a bit of publicity that served us well in future recruiting of students.

"Maestro Nicholas Harsanyi. . .led the 1971 summer session in the twin capacity of conductor and administrative director."

34

As if to bless all our efforts, the evening of August 12 turned out to be dazzling. The sky was of that specially deep satin blue that you find exclusively in the Mediterranean world, and only the soft illumination of the piazza itself could compete with that of the moon and the stars. The air was cool and still enough not to rustle a page of music. Even before the program began, we had an overflow audience.

The concert went off without a hitch, and with each new composition, I noticed that there were more and more people crowding into the piazza. At the conclusion of the program there must have been 2,000 or 3,000 people on hand, many of them standing on the twin staircases that gracefully curl down from the Palace of Senators onto the piazza below. The applause which greeted the final work, Aaron Copland's *Appalachian Spring Suite*, was so insistent and prolonged that an encore was in order.

August 12, 1970: "Even before the program began we had an overflow audience."

Knowing that conductor Gottlieb barely had had time to prepare his musicians for the music on the program (much less encores), I expected to see him motion the orchestra off stage. To my surprise, he gestured instead to a musician in the last row, to whom he passed the baton.

The young man in question was a young trumpeter and composer named Gary Buchanan, from Sanford, North Carolina, who gratified the audience's wish for more music by conducting his own *Sections for Oboe and Orchestra* — an eight- or ten-minute composition that provoked applause even more ecstatic than before. The evening was a total triumph!

Not the least pleased among the public was the normally reserved Ambassador Martin, who now warmly expressed the desire to talk with some of his fellow North Carolinians in the orchestra. This was easy enough to arrange, there being several dozen on hand, and soon enough the fast-emptying piazza was filled with the inimitable dulcet tones of southerners greeting one another.

I have always regarded that August evening in Rome as the epitome of all that we have been striving for with our program. More exactly, the concert was a perfect microcosm of the whole adventure abroad. First of all, there was the fact of putting together a program and rushing to prepare it in time. Another familiar element was the necessity of close collaboration with the Italians, without whose help and constant sympathy our program would have floundered in its first year. Equally characteristic was the high level of performance and the generous response of our listeners.

Lastly — and this has been a conscious theme throughout these pages — there was a strong element of destiny. Had the applause not been so great, Gottlieb would not have been prompted to the generous gesture of passing the baton. But he <u>did</u> pass it, and young Buchanan thus came to conduct his own music, in a piazza designed by Michelangelo, before a public of thousands. Who can measure what this meant to him?

APPENDIX A

Siena Summer Session Faculty and Staff, 1967-1972

1967

STAFF

Artistic Director	Giorgio Ciompi
Executive Assistant	Franco Agostini
Assistant to the Director	Julia Mueller
Secretary	Mary Manus

FACULTY

Orchestral Conductor	Piero Bellugi
Piano	Olegna Fuschi, Howard Aibel
Voice	Rose Bampton
Violin	Marc Gottlieb
Viola	Aldo Bennici
Cello	Pietro Grossi
Double Bass	Alfredo Brandi
Flute, Piccolo	Pier Mencarelli
Oboe, English Horn	Federico De Sanctis
Clarinet	Detalmo Cornetti
Bassoon	Umberto Mazzuccato
Horn	Pasqualino Rossi
Trumpet	Angelo Massini
Trombone, Tuba	Benito Mungai
Harp	Egle Scorpioni
Composition	Roman Vlad
Theory	Thomas Pasatieri
Italian Language	Frances Rello

1968

STAFF

Artistic Director	Giorgio Ciompi
Executive Assistant	Franco Agostini
Assistant to the Director	Julia Mueller
Dean of Men	Thomas Kenan
Dean of Women	Frances Rello
Secretary	Mary Manus

FACULTY

Orchestral Conductor	Piero Bellugi
French Horn	Frederick Bergstone
Vocal Coach	Paul Berl
History of Italian Art	Marianna Jenkins
Voice	Norman Farrow
Italian Language	Francesco Gulli
Cello	Irving Klein
Composition	Roman Vlad
Piano	Vincenzo Vitale
Organ	Alessandro Esposito

1969

STAFF

Artistic Director	Giorgio Ciompi
Assistant to the Director	Paolo Olsoufieff
Staff Assistant	H. Alan Sims
Dean of Men	William Baskin
Dean of Women	Gerd Young
Secretary	Mary Manus

FACULTY

Orchestral Conductor	Gaetano Delogu
Chamber Music Faculty:	
Strings	Irving Klein, Jerry Horner
Clarinet	Robert Listokin
Coach-Accompanist	Margo Garrett
Coach-Accompanist	Donald Nold
Voice	Rose Bampton
Guitar	Jesus Silva

1970

STAFF

Administrative Director	William Baskin
Assistant to the Director	Paolo Olsoufieff
Press, Publicity	Eugene Rizzo
Dean of Men	Jean Ramseyer
Dean of Women	Gerd Young
Secretary	Ruth Toolin

38

FACULTY

Orchestral Conductor	Marc Gottlieb
Chamber Music Faculty:	
Strings	Irving Klein
Strings	Vartan Manoogian
Strings	Jerry Horner
Strings	Marc Gottlieb
Flute	Philip Dunigan
Choral Conductor	Philippe Buhler

1971

STAFF

General Director	Nicholas Harsanyi
Assistant to the Director	Jean Ramseyer
Press, Publicity, Booking	Eugene Rizzo
Italian Liaison	Galliano Passerini
Dean of Men	David Wilson
Dean of Women	Mary Wilson
Secretary	Dawne Alstrom

FACULTY

Orchestral Conductor	Nicholas Harsanyi
Assistant to the Conductor	Byron Hanson
Chamber Music Faculty:	
Strings	Riccardo Brengola
Strings	Vartan Manoogian
Woodwinds	Severino Gazzelloni
Brass	Frederick Bergstone
Voice	Janice Harsanyi
Guitar	Jesus Silva
Harp	Patricia Pence
Choral Conductor	Philippe Buhler

1972

STAFF

General Director	Nicholas Harsanyi
Manager	Eugene Rizzo
Assistant to the Manager	Galliano Passerini
Dean of Men	Alton Busby

Dean of Women	Betty C. Masten
Secretary	Anna-Paola Bartolini

FACULTY

Orchestral Conductor	Nicholas Harsanyi
Chamber Music Faculty:	
Strings	Vartan Manoogian
Strings	Franco Gulli
Strings	Janos Starker
Woodwinds	Severino Gazzelloni
Woodwinds	Giuseppe Garbarino
Brass	Robert Nagle
Guitar	Jesus Silva
Voice	Janice Harsanyi
Coach-Accompanist	Margo Garrett

APPENDIX B

Some Graduates of the NCSA Program Abroad
1967-72

It is highly gratifying to see that so many of our graduates of the summer sessions abroad have already made significant progress in the world of music. I say "already" because the entire history of the program spans only six years; in most cases, even our oldest graduates are barely twenty-five years of age.

It is neither my intention nor within my powers to compile "alumni notes" that in any way pretend to be complete. As elsewhere in these sketches, I have deliberately chosen specific cases and left the reader to imagine for himself the general picture. Many of our students — the course of their careers unknown to me as I write now — may be making even more signal contributions than those I have troubled to chronicle here.

One more note. If I do not delude myself thinking that the "Siena experience" was of utmost importance in the lives of all these musicians, neither do I underestimate its significance. Most of our alumni with whom I have talked have expressed positive reactions to the program. Some spoke of a decisive encounter with a new teacher, others of the stimulus afforded by a country steeped in musical tradition. All of them admitted to the intense excitement of coming in contact with new standards, new values, new audiences. Now on to our capsule biographies.

Georgyn Geetlin, *soprano,* came from the North Carolina School of the Arts to participate in the 1967 and 1969 Siena sessions. In 1970 she returned to Italy and took part in the Opera Barga program. She is the recipient of a William Matheus Sullivan Musical Foundation grant (1970), and has sung in Town Hall and Alice Tully Hall at Lincoln Center. She has appeared on Broadway in the role of the opera singer in "Two Gentlemen of Verona."

Margo Garrett, *pianist,* came as a student to Siena in 1967 and again in 1969. A graduate of the North Carolina School of the Arts, she is now on the faculty at Juilliard while simultaneously taking a master's degree in accompaniment at the Manhattan School of Music. She played in Town Hall in November of 1972, and has appeared widely as accompanist for such soloists as Shirley Love, Seth McCoy, and Janice Harsanyi.

Romuald Tecco, *violinist,* is now the concert master of the St. Paul Chamber Orchestra. A graduate of Juilliard, he attended the first two Siena sessions in 1967 and 1968. Tecco has been on the faculty of the Manhattan School, a teaching-fellow at Juilliard, and artist-in-residence at Temple University. He has recorded for Phillips, RCA, and CRI. This March he was violin soloist, under the direction of Aaron Copland, in a performance of music by Darius Milhaud to honor the eightieth birthday of that composer.

Alfred C. Morris, *conductor,* came from the Mannes College of Music to participate in the 1968 and 1969 summer sessions. He won second prize in the *AIDEM conducting competition in Florence, later continuing his studies with Franco Ferrara at Rome's Santa Cecilia Conservatory. Morris is now a member of the faculty of the State University of New York at Binghamton, where he conducts chorus and orchestra.

Phil Wachowski, *violist,* was enrolled in three summer sessions: 1969, 1970, and 1972. Now a fellowship student at the North Carolina School of the Arts, he is also a member of the Piedmont Chamber Orchestra. Last winter he took part in the Christmas String Seminar conducted by Alexander Schneider, concluding with a December 29 concert in Carnegie Hall.

Kon Woo Paik, *pianist,* is building a major career as a soloist. His all-Ravel recital last November 27 at Tully Hall in New York prompted Raymond Ericson to write in the *New York Times* that "few pianists today would be superior in sustaining interest throughout such a program. . . . Paik has a fluid, graceful technique, which made the taxing music seem to flow effortlessly from his fingers." The young Korean pianist studied at Juilliard and participated in the first North Carolina School of the Arts Siena Session, 1967.

Giuseppe De Rugeriis, *conductor,* is assistant to Gian Carlo Menotti and conducted on two occasions at the 1972 Spoleto Festival. A graduate of Mannes (1967), he took part in the 1969 summer session, subsequently continuing studies in Rome with Franco Ferrara. Recipient of an Alice M. Ditson Award, De Rugeriis was also chairman of the music department at the Overseas International High School in Rome. Prior to making his conducting debut at Spoleto, he was assistant to Thomas Schippers and Christopher Keene.

Kathleen Lenski, *violinist,* took part in the 1968 and 1969 summer sessions, later entering the Chigiana master classes of Maestro Franco Gulli. Under his coaching, she was encouraged to enter the Paganini Competitions in Genoa, where she placed second.

Kimberly Schmidt, *pianist,* made his solo debut last December 17 at Orchestra Hall in Chicago. Now studying with Cyril Smith at the Royal College of Music in London, Schmidt is an Eastman graduate who participated in the 1972 North Carolina School of the Arts summer session.

William Henry, *violinist,* is a member of the Raphael Trio. A graduate of the University of Southern California and the Juilliard School, he took part in the 1968 summer session. Currently on the faculty of the Friends Academy of New York, Henry has been a featured soloist both on WQXR radio and on WNYC-TV.

---

*AIDEM (Associazione Italiana Diffusione Educazione Musicale: Italian Association for Musical Education)

APPENDIX C

Directory of Students, 1967-72

1967

Name	Instrument	College or Conservatory
Alicea, Mercedes	Voice	Manhattan School of Music, New York, N. Y.
Ashe, Dan	Horn	North Carolina School of the Arts Winston-Salem, N. C.
Bair, Edward J., Jr.	Voice	Messiah College, Graham, Pa.
Barrow, Rebecca	Piano	North Carolina School of the Arts Winston-Salem, N. C.
Basquin, Peter	Piano	Manhattan School of Music New York, N. Y.
Ben-Uri, Shalom	Violin	North Carolina Symphony Chapel Hill, N. C.
Bieler, Ida	Violin	North Carolina School of the Arts Winston-Salem, N. C.
Bland, Virginia	Oboe	Juilliard School of Music New York, N. Y.
Butt, James	Piano	North Carolina School of the Arts Winston-Salem, N. C.
Byers, Patrick	Piano	North Carolina School of the Arts Winston-Salem, N. C.
Byrnes, James	Trumpet	Newark College of Engineering Newark, N. J.
Califano, Constance	Piano	Pembroke College, Providence, R. I.
Case, Neely Maude	Viola	Ohio State University Columbus, Ohio
Chudy, Natalie	Voice	Manhattan School of Music New York, N. Y.
Ciompi, Arturo	Clarinet	North Carolina School of the Arts Winston-Salem, N. C.
Clark, Cynthia	Piano	University of North Carolina Chapel Hill, N. C.
Clark, Robert	Piano	Cornell, Ithaca, N. Y.
Clausen, Jeanne	Violin	Sarah Lawrence College Bronxville, N. Y.
Colina, Michael	Composition	North Carolina School of the Arts Winston-Salem, N. C.
Conant, Ida	Voice	North Carolina School of the Arts Winston-Salem, N. C.
Cooper, Rex	Piano	Oberlin Conservatory of Music Oberlin, Ohio

Croley, Randell	Composition	University of Louisville Louisville, Ky.
Davis, Deborah	Cello	North Carolina School of the Arts Winston-Salem, N. C.
Donovetsky, Gregory	Oboe	—
Efland, Barbara	Voice	North Carolina School of the Arts Winston-Salem, N. C.
Ellis, Van Zandt	Piano	Manhattan School of Music New York, N. Y.
Epperson, John	Horn	North Carolina School of the Arts Winston-Salem, N. C.
Gardner, Kay	Viola	Manhattan School of Music New York, N. Y.
Garrett, Margo	Piano	North Carolina School of the Arts Winston-Salem, N. C.
Gates, Keith	Composition	North Carolina School of the Arts Winston-Salem, N. C.
Geetlein, Georgyn	Voice	North Carolina School of the Arts Winston-Salem, N. C.
Geller, Michael	Bass	Indiana University Bloomington, Ind.
Geoghegan, Ivy	Violin	University of North Carolina Chapel Hill, N. C.
Giannini, Maura	Violin	North Carolina School of the Arts Winston-Salem, N. C.
Glenn, Bonita	Voice	Philadelphia Musical Academy Philadelphia, Pa.
Glick, David	Clarinet	Carnegie Institute of Technology Pittsburgh, Pa.
Goldstein, Lauren	Bassoon	Temple University Philadelphia, Pa.
Gowan, Pamela	Piano	North Carolina School of the Arts Winston-Salem, N. C.
Griffin, Robert	Piano	University of North Carolina Chapel Hill, N. C.
Groshong, Geoffry	Oboe	Eastman School of Music Rochester, N. Y.
Haff, Harold	Trombone	Montclair State College Upper Montclair, N. J.
Harrelson, Patricia	Voice	North Carolina School of the Arts Winston-Salem, N. C.
Harris, Daniel	Bass	Eastern Kentucky University Richmond, Ky.
Hochberg, Gertrude	Cello	North Carolina Symphony Chapel Hill, N. C.
Holoman, Kern	Bassoon	Duke University, Durham, N. C.
Inman, Joseph	Percussion	University of Illinois Urbana, Ill.

Jones, Nell	Piano	University of North Carolina Chapel Hill, N. C.
Julian, Jonathan	Clarinet	North Carolina School of the Arts Winston-Salem, N. C.
Klavins, Eriks	Violin	North Carolina Symphony Chapel Hill, N. C.
Klein, Phillip	Viola	Eastman School of Music Rochester, N. Y.
Knipper, Gail	Clarinet	Manhattan School of Music New York, N. Y.
Kuehn, David	Trumpet	Juilliard School of Music New York, N. Y.
La Monaco, Neal	Cello	University of Rochester Rochester, N. Y.
Lattimore, Martha	Voice	Westminster Choir College Princeton, N. J.
Laube, Marguerite	Viola	Eastern Kentucky University Richmond, Ky.
Levine, David	Piano	Manhattan School of Music New York, N. Y.
Lindsay, Martha	Voice	Madison College Harrisonburg, Va.
Little, Myra Elizabeth	Horn	Capital University Columbus, Ohio
Martin, Thomas	Piano	North Carolina School of the Arts Winston-Salem, N. C.
Mazer, Susan	Harp	Wayne State University Detroit, Mich.
Meyer, Jonathan	Flute	Columbia University New York, N. Y.
Miller, Sandra	Flute	North Carolina School of the Arts Winston-Salem, N. C.
Miura, Naoyuki	Bass	Manhattan School of Music New York, N. Y.
Morganstern, Mark	Bass	North Carolina School of the Arts Winston-Salem, N. C.
Moss, Bruce	Piano	North Carolina School of the Arts Winston-Salem, N. C.
Moss, Linda	Viola	Eastman School of Music Rochester, N. Y.
Nakashima, Rieko	Piano	North Carolina School of the Arts Winston-Salem, N. C.
Nussbaum, Charles	Bassoon	Juilliard School of Music New York, N. Y.
Okamura, Kineko	Violin	Manhattan School of Music New York, N. Y.
Olsen, Susan	Violin	Manhattan School of Music New York, N. Y.

45

Pace, Cynthia	Piano	Horace Greely High School Mt. Kisco, N. Y.
Paik, Kon Woo	Piano	Juilliard School of Music New York, N. Y.
Parker, Suzanne	Violin	University of North Carolina Chapel Hill, N. C.
Parkhurst, Charles	Conducting	Duke University Durham, N. C.
Peeler, Elizabeth	Voice	North Carolina School of the Arts Winston-Salem, N. C.
Pendergast, William Jeff	Percussion	Duke University Durham, N. C.
Perrone, Janis	Piano	North Carolina School of the Arts Winston-Salem, N. C.
Perry, Henry	Trombone	Duke University Durham, N. C.
Pietracatella, Dorothy	Voice	Manhattan School of Music New York, N. Y.
Pittman, Dorothy	Voice	Converse College Spartanburg, S. C.
Plexico, Sandra	Voice	North Carolina School of the Arts Winston-Salem, N. C.
Pliler, Richard	Violin	Texas Christian University Fort Worth, Tex.
Plylar, John Russell	Trumpet	North Carolina School of the Arts Winston-Salem, N. C.
Price, Virginia	Violin	North Carolina School of the Arts Winston-Salem, N. C.
Rendleman, Ruth	Piano	North Carolina School of the Arts Winston-Salem, N. C.
Ricci, Riana	Violin	Eastman School of Music Rochester, N. Y.
Roden, Wayne	Viola	North Carolina School of the Arts Winston-Salem, N. C.
Rose, Bernard	Piano	Juilliard School of Music New York, N. Y.
Rudisill, Cheryl	Piano	North Carolina School of the Arts Winston-Salem, N. C.
Schoenfeld, Max	Flute	Manhattan School of Music New York, N. Y.
Schwartz, Nathan	Bassoon	University of Pennsylvania Philadelphia, Pa.
Scott, Lauren	Cello	Indiana University Bloomington, Ind.
Shakespeare, Margaret	Violin	Juilliard School of Music New York, N. Y.
Sherrill, Steve	Trombone	North Carolina School of the Arts Winston-Salem, N. C.

46

Sherry, Fred	Cello	Juilliard School of Music New York, N. Y.
Sizemore, John	Tuba	North Carolina School of the Arts Winston-Salem, N. C.
Smith, Joseph	Piano	North Carolina School of the Arts Winston-Salem, N. C.
Spearman, Andrew	Horn	University of Connecticut Storrs, Conn.
Starr, Roland	Horn	Eastman School of Music Rochester, N. Y.
Suarez, Thomas	Violin	Valley Stream Central High School Long Island, N. Y.
Tait, Margaret	Cello	North Carolina School of the Arts Winston-Salem, N. C.
Teachey, Martha	Voice	North Carolina School of the Arts Winston-Salem, N. C.
Teco, Romauld	Violin	Juilliard School of Music New York, N. Y.
Tichman, Nina	Piano	Barnard College New York, N. Y.
Topilow, Carl	Clarinet	Manhattan School of Music New York, N. Y.
Trexler, Ruth	Cello	Southern Methodist University Dallas, Tex.
Troxler, Rebecca	Flute	North Carolina School of the Arts Winston-Salem, N. C.
Turner, Marian	Violin	University of North Carolina Chapel Hill, N. C.
Ujcich, Randy	Bass	Curtis Institute of Music Philadelphia, Pa.
Varney, Jan Paul	Viola	Eastern Kentucky University Richmond, Ky.
Vodnoy, Robert	Conducting	North Carolina School of the Arts Winston-Salem, N. C.
Waddell, Charles	Horn	Muskingum College New Concord, Ohio
Wasserman, Ellen	Piano	Utah State University Salt Lake City, Utah
Williams, John	Voice	North Carolina School of the Arts Winston-Salem, N. C.
Wilson, Randy	Flute	North Carolina School of the Arts Winston-Salem, N. C.
Wolf, Laura	Flute	Eastman School of Music Rochester, N. Y.
Wolf, Margy Lu	Violin	Eastman School of Music Rochester, N. Y.
Woodhams, Richard	Oboe	Curtis Institute of Music Philadelphia, Pa.

1968

Aiello, Theresa	Flute	Juilliard School of Music New York, N. Y.
Anstadt, Ronald Lee	Piano	Manhattan School of Music New York, N. Y.
Barrow, Rebecca	Piano	North Carolina School of the Arts Winston-Salem, N. C.
Belchetz, Ruth	Violin	Oberlin College Oberlin, Ohio
Bernhardt, Lynn R., Jr.	Percussion	North Carolina School of the Arts Winston-Salem, N. C.
Beu, Sally	Cello	North Carolina School of the Arts Winston-Salem, N. C.
Borda, Deborah	Viola	New England Conservatory Boston, Mass.
Bouldin, James W., III	Horn	North Carolina School of the Arts Winston-Salem, N. C.
Bowman, Alan	Tuba	North Carolina School of the Arts Winston-Salem, N. C.
Bradley, Lea	Piano	North Carolina School of the Arts Winston-Salem, N. C.
Brown, Paul G.	Horn	North Carolina School of the Arts Winston-Salem, N. C.
Chapman, Lucy	Violin	North Carolina School of the Arts Winston-Salem, N. C.
Cheek, John	Voice	North Carolina School of the Arts Winston-Salem, N. C.
Ciompi, Arturo	Clarinet	North Carolina School of the Arts Winston-Salem, N. C.
Cohen, Susan	Cello	Juilliard School of Music New York, N. Y.
Colina, Michael	Composition	North Carolina School of the Arts Winston-Salem, N. C.
Cordle, Andrew	Bassoon	North Carolina School of the Arts Winston-Salem, N. C.
Cowperthwaite, Cathie	Trumpet	University of Michigan Ann Arbor, Mich.
Critchley, Ruther	Viola	North Carolina School of the Arts Winston-Salem, N. C.
Cunningham, Robert	Piano	Duke University Durham, N. C.
Curry, Barbara	Voice	North Carolina School of the Arts Winston-Salem, N. C.
Cutts, Ella	Voice	North Carolina School of the Arts Winston-Salem, N. C.
Davis, Miles	Bass	Belmont High School Dayton, Ohio

Decatur, Douglas	Voice	North Carolina School of the Arts Winston-Salem, N. C.
Dion, John F.	Horn	University of Louisville Louisville, Ky.
Dixon, Geraldine	Voice	Radford College. Radford, Va.
Egbers, Kathie M.	Oboe	Portland Symphony Orchestra Portland, Oreg.
Ellis, Randy	Oboe	North Carolina School of the Arts Winston-Salem, N. C.
Fennimore, Linda Dale	Violin	Manhattan School of Music New York, N. Y.
Fisher, Robert James	Oboe	Juilliard School of Music New York, N. Y.
Furiness, Dennis	Piano	Manhattan School of Music New York, N. Y.
Gardner, James E., Jr.	Trumpet	North Carolina School of the Arts Winston-Salem, N. C.
Gedzelman, Jack	Piano	Queens College, Flushing, N. Y.
Gerber, Stephen R.	Composition	Columbia University New York, N. Y.
Giannini, Ferruccio	Viola	North Carolina School of the Arts Winston-Salem, N. C.
Gilbert, Joan	Piano	Juilliard School of Music New York, N. Y.
Graham, Jane	Organ	North Carolina School of the Arts Winston-Salem, N. C.
Green, Donald	Cello	Mannes College New York, N. Y.
Habig, Dorothy K.	Horn	Manhattan School of Music New York, N. Y.
Harris, Fay L.	Voice	St. Augustine's College Raleigh, N. C.
Hauck, Betty	Viola	Brandeis University Waltham, Mass.
Henry, C. William	Violin	Juilliard School of Music New York, N. Y.
Hines, Laurie	Clarinet	North Carolina School of the Arts Winston-Salem, N. C.
Holmes, Sharon	Violin	University of Michigan Ann Arbor, Mich.
Holoman, D. Kern	Conducting	Duke University Durham, N. C.
Julian, Jonathan	Clarinet	North Carolina School of the Arts Winston-Salem, N. C.
Kephart, Sam	Viola	North Carolina School of the Arts Winston-Salem, N. C.
Kollath, Lana	Piano	Saint Lawrence University Canton, N. Y.

Lagosky, Karen Ann	Conducting	Temple University Philadelphia, Pa.
Lamneck, Ester	Clarinet	North Carolina School of the Arts Winston-Salem, N. C.
Lane, Betty	Voice	Juilliard School of Music New York, N. Y.
Lawrence, Thomas Paul	Voice	North Carolina School of the Arts Winston-Salem, N. C.
Lenski, Kathleen	Violin	Juilliard School of Music New York, N. Y.
Litaker, Donald	Voice	North Carolina School of the Arts Winston-Salem, N. C.
McCraw, Michael	Bassoon	North Carolina School of the Arts Winston-Salem, N. C.
Millhouse, Ruth	Viola	Manhattan School of Music New York, N. Y.
Moorman, Wilson O., III	Percussion	—
Morganstern, Mark	Bass	North Carolina School of the Arts Winston-Salem, N. C.
Morris, Alfred C.	Conducting	Mannes College New York, N. Y.
Nield, Christine	Flute	North Carolina School of the Arts Winston-Salem, N. C.
Olarte, Martha	Trumpet	North Carolina School of the Arts Winston-Salem, N. C.
Peeler, Elizabeth	Voice	North Carolina School of the Arts Winston-Salem, N. C.
Peters, Lynn	Bass	Indiana University, Bloomington, Ind.
Pobanz, Marsha	Piano	North Carolina School of the Arts Winston-Salem, N. C.
Redding, Frances S.	Voice	University of North Carolina Chapel Hill, N. C.
Rice, Robert Scott	Viola	North Carolina School of the Arts Winston-Salem, N. C.
Robinson, Sharon	Cello	North Carolina School of the Arts Winston-Salem, N. C.
Roden, Inez	Cello	North Carolina School of the Arts Winston-Salem, N. C.
Sanders, Sylvia	Harp	Birmingham Southern College Birmingham, Ala.
Scelba, Anthony	Bass	Manhattan School of Music New York, N. Y.
Senter, Anthony M.	Organ	North Carolina School of the Arts Winston-Salem, N. C.
Seplow, Kathy	Violin	Juilliard School of Music New York, N. Y.
Shapiro, Madeleine	Cello	Roslyn High School Long Island, N. Y.

Sherrill, Steve	Trombone	North Carolina School of the Arts Winston-Salem, N. C.
Shumate, Don	Trombone	University of Louisville Louisville, Ky.
Smith, Joseph	Piano	North Carolina School of the Arts Winston-Salem, N. C.
Sokol, Anne	Violin	University of Washington Seattle, Wash.
Spindler, John	Violin	Bergenfield High School Bergenfield, N. J.
Stell, Marcia	Violin	North Carolina School of the Arts Winston-Salem, N. C.
Stout, David G.	Trombone	Eastman School of Music Rochester, N. Y.
Strong, Jane E.	Piano	Vassar College Poughkeepsie, N. Y.
Suarez, Tom	Violin	Juilliard School of Music New York, N. Y.
Sylvester, Vicki	Violin	Juilliard School of Music New York, N. Y.
Szekely, Eva D.	Violin	Juilliard School of Music New York, N. Y.
Teco, Romuald	Violin	Juilliard School of Music New York, N. Y.
Thacker, Bernard	Voice	North Carolina School of the Arts Winston-Salem, N. C.
Tillman, David Jonathan	Bassoon	North Carolina School of the Arts Winston-Salem, N. C.
Tuton, Bobby	Bass	North Carolina School of the Arts Winston-Salem, N. C.
Tyson, Hal	Piano	North Carolina School of the Arts Winston-Salem, N. C.
Tyson, Margaret	Violin	Texas Christian University Fort Worth, Tex.
Vodnoy, Robert	Conducting	North Carolina School of the Arts Winston-Salem, N. C.
Vreeland, Sue	Viola	University of Michigan Ann Arbor, Mich.
Walker, Susan	Cello	North Carolina School of the Arts Winston-Salem, N. C.
Ward, Mark	Cello	North Carolina School of the Arts Winston-Salem, N. C.
Weintrob, Neil E.	Violin	Temple University Philadelphia, Pa.
Werts, Dan	Composition	Princeton University Princeton, N. J.
Whitener, Carolyn Sue	Horn	Appalachian State University Boone, N. C.

Wilson, Ransom	Flute	North Carolina School of the Arts Winston-Salem, N. C.
Wincenz, Carol	Flute	Oberlin College Oberlin, Ohio
Witcraft, Derek R.	Organ	North Carolina School of the Arts Winston-Salem, N. C.

1969

Albert, Judith Marion	Voice	Brooklyn College Brooklyn, N. Y.
Alderman, Jean E.	Viola	Duke University, Durham, N. C.
Anderson, Shari	Voice	—
Avril, Franck	Oboe	Augusta Prep School Augusta, Ga.
Ball, Marilyn	Voice	North Carolina School of the Arts Winston-Salem, N. C.
Bannon, Peter	Trombone	Hartt College Philadelphia, Pa.
Barbee, Vincent	Horn	North Carolina School of the Arts Winston-Salem, N. C.
Berger, Francine	Flute	Indiana University Bloomington, Ind.
Bodemann, Thomas	Violin	—
Brackens, Lynn Ellen	Voice	—
Bradley, Lea	Piano	North Carolina School of the Arts Winston-Salem, N. C.
Braunstein, Sheila	Viola	State University of New York Buffalo, N. Y.
Brown, Joshua	Guitar	North Carolina School of the Arts Winston-Salem, N. C.
Bucchianeri, Marcia	Violin	North Carolina School of the Arts Winston-Salem, N. C.
Buchanan, Gary	Trumpet	North Carolina School of the Arts Winston-Salem, N. C.
Bumgarner, Thomas Stanley	Guitar	Lenoir Rhyne College Hickory, N. C.
Bunch, Benjamin D.	Guitar	North Carolina School of the Arts Winston-Salem, N. C.
Burton, Barbara J.	Percussion	—
Calderon, Javiar	Guitar	North Carolina School of the Arts Winston-Salem, N. C.
Carroll, James E.	Bass	Juilliard School of Music New York, N. Y.
Chapman, John David	Trombone	North Carolina School of the Arts Winston-Salem, N. C.

Cheek, John	Voice	North Carolina School of the Arts Winston-Salem, N. C.
Christopher, Barbara	Voice	—
Ciompi, Arturo	Clarinet	North Carolina School of the Arts Winston-Salem, N. C.
Cohen, Susan	Cello	Juilliard School of Music New York, N. Y.
Cole, Lynn	Piano	University of North Carolina Chapel Hill, N. C.
Collier, Robert W., III	Tuba	North Carolina School of the Arts Winston-Salem, N. C.
Cowan, Carole, L.	Violin	Yale University New Haven, Conn.
Critchley, Ruth	Viola	North Carolina School of the Arts Winston-Salem, N. C.
Davis, Chris	Voice	—
Decatur, Douglas	Voice	North Carolina School of the Arts Winston-Salem, N. C.
Decker, Margaret L.	Cello	Juilliard School of Music New York, N. Y.
De Rugeriis, Joseph Carmen	Conducting	Columbia University New York, N. Y.
Despalj, Valter	Cello	Juilliard School of Music New York, N. Y.
Dietz, Laura	Flute	North Carolina School of the Arts Winston-Salem, N. C.
Edwards, Linda	Piano	North Carolina School of the Arts Winston-Salem, N. C.
Efland, Barbara	Voice	Manhattan School of Music New York, N. Y.
Eicher, Paul S.	Bass	Indiana University, Bloomington, Ind.
Ellis, George Randall	Oboe	North Carolina School of the Arts Winston-Salem, N. C.
Esaki, Katsuko	Violin	—
Fiene, Paul Rene	Guitar	North Carolina School of the Arts Winston-Salem, N. C.
Finkelstein, Thelma	Voice	Manhattan School of Music New York, N. Y.
Fletcher, James	Guitar	North Carolina School of the Arts Winston-Salem, N. C.
Foster, Edward	Trombone	Hartt College Philadelphia, Pa.
Fusco, E. Miles	Piano	Juilliard School of Music New York, N. Y.
Garrett, Margo	Piano	North Carolina School of the Arts Winston-Salem, N. C.
Gates, Keith	Composition	North Carolina School of the Arts Winston-Salem, N. C.

Geetlein, Georgyn	Voice	North Carolina School of the Arts Winston-Salem, N. C.
Green, Donald	Cello	New England Conservatory Boston, Mass.
Greitzer, Deborah	Violin	Sarah Lawrence College Bronxville, N. Y.
Grier, Robert J., Jr.	Trumpet	North Carolina School of the Arts Winston-Salem, N. C.
Hansen, Marcus F.	Guitar	North Carolina School of the Arts Winston-Salem, N. C.
Harada, Sadao	Cello	—
Henry, Deborah	Oboe	North Carolina School of the Arts Winston-Salem, N. C.
Hightower, Gail	Bassoon	Manhattan School of Music New York, N. Y.
Houser, Thomas Henri	Horn	Juilliard School of Music New York, N. Y.
Howell, Thomas	Horn	Juilliard School of Music New York, N. Y.
Isomura, Kazuhide	Violin	Juilliard School of Music New York, N. Y.
Julian, Jonathan	Clarinet	North Carolina School of the Arts Winston-Salem, N. C.
Kanoff, Ronni	Violin	Juilliard School of Music New York, N. Y.
Kennedy, John D.	Violin	Juilliard School of Music New York, N. Y.
Kreger, James	Cello	Juilliard School of Music New York, N. Y.
Kuderna, Jerry	Piano	San Francisco Conservatory San Francisco, Calif.
Lamneck, Ester	Clarinet	North Carolina School of the Arts Winston-Salem, N. C.
Lane, Betty	Voice	Juilliard School of Music New York, N. Y.
Lazarus, Leonard	Clarinet	State University of New York Buffalo, N. Y.
Ledbetter, Judy	Violin	University of North Carolina Chapel Hill, N. C.
Leiderman, Judith	Flute	Brown University, Providence, R. I.
Lenski, Kathleen	Violin	Juilliard School of Music New York, N. Y.
Light, Susan	Violin	Interlochen Arts Academy Interlochen, Mich.
Litaker, Donald	Voice	North Carolina School of the Arts Winston-Salem, N. C.
Litven, David	Violin	University of Michigan Ann Arbor, Mich.

Magnuson, Phil	Viola	Duke University, Durham, N. C.
Mason, S. Douglas	Horn	North Carolina School of the Arts Winston-Salem, N. C.
Maul, Eric	Bassoon	North Carolina School of the Arts Winston-Salem, N. C.
Mazer, Susan	Harp	Stanford University Stanford, Calif.
Meyerrieks, Jeffrey	Guitar	North Carolina School of the Arts Winston-Salem, N. C.
Milbourne, Omega	Voice	Juilliard School of Music New York, N. Y.
Miller, Sandra	Flute	Curtis Institute of Music Philadelphia, Pa.
Mingus, Richard	Horn	Oberlin College Oberlin, Ohio
Moorman, Wilson	Percussion	Juilliard School of Music New York, N. Y.
Morris, Alfred C.	Conducting	Mannes College New York, N. Y.
Morris, Harold	Guitar	Mannes College New York, N. Y.
Moser, Joan	Horn	Herricks High School Long Island, N. Y.
Neumann, Susan	Violin	Juilliard School of Music New York, N. Y.
Oppens, Ursula	Piano	Juilliard School of Music New York, N. Y.
Perry, David	Guitar	North Carolina School of the Arts Winston-Salem, N. C.
Polivnick, Paul	Conducting	Juilliard School of Music New York, N. Y.
Pologe, Steven	Cello	Teaneck High School Teaneck, N. J.
Provenza, Salvatore D.	Voice	Juilliard School of Music New York, N. Y.
Rabiner, Lois	Voice	—
Randolph, Laurie	Guitar	North Carolina School of the Arts Winston-Salem, N. C.
Riera, Ana	Voice	Manhattan School of Music New York, N. Y.
Roden, Ruth	Bassoon	North Carolina School of the Arts Winston-Salem, N. C.
Rose, Bernard	Piano	Juilliard School of Music New York, N. Y.
Samson, Michel	Conducting	Mannes College New York, N. Y.
Scheer, Valerie	Violin	Wichita State University Witchita, Kans.

55

Scrutchfield, Russell W.	Trumpet	University of Kansas Lawrence, Kans.
Senter, Anthony M.	Organ	North Carolina School of the Arts Winston-Salem, N. C.
Sippel, Andrea Dori	Viola	SUNY College at Potsdam Potsdam, N. Y.
Sirota, Elissa	Viola	Queens College Flushing, N. Y.
Snapp, Shannon	Cello	North Carolina School of the Arts Winston-Salem, N. C.
Sokol, Anne	Violin	University of Washington Seattle, Wash.
Sorton, Robert	Oboe	North Carolina School of the Arts Winston-Salem, N. C.
Stein, Charles	Guitar	North Carolina School of the Arts Winston-Salem, N. C.
Strahl, Dorothy	Violin	—
Sublette, Pleas E.	Guitar	Eastern New Mexico University Portales, N. Mex.
Thoreson, Thomas	Bass	New England Conservatory Boston, Mass.
Trachtenberg, Alta	Voice	Manhattan School of Music New York, N. Y.
Twerdowsky, Paul	Guitar	Teaneck High School Teaneck, N. J.
Wachowski, Phil	Viola	North Carolina School of the Arts Winston-Salem, N. C.
Wagner, Joanne	Bass	Indiana University Bloomington, Ind.
Ward, Mark	Cello	North Carolina School of the Arts Winston-Salem, N. C.
Ward, Timothy	Bassoon	North Carolina School of the Arts Winston-Salem, N. C.
Westafter, George	Guitar	North Carolina School of the Arts Winston-Salem, N. C.
Williams, Delbert Lee	Bass	Ohio State University Columbus, Ohio
Young, Barbara Louise	Voice	Manhattan School of Music New York, N. Y.

1970

Arpaia, Gabriel	Clarinet	North Carolina School of the Arts Winston-Salem, N. C.
Ashe, Dan	Horn	North Carolina School of the Arts Winston-Salem, N. C.

Ashe, Margaret	Cello	North Carolina School of the Arts Winston-Salem, N. C.
Barbee, Vincent	Horn	North Carolina School of the Arts Winston-Salem, N. C.
Barrow, Rebecca	Piano	North Carolina School of the Arts Winston-Salem, N. C.
Biondo, Gino	Bass	Manhattan School of Music New York, N. Y.
Blair, Sidney	Trombone	Wayne State University Detroit, Mich.
Bono, Betsy	Violin	Thomas Jefferson High School Richmond, Va.
Braunstein, Sheila	Viola	Buffalo State Buffalo, N. Y.
Brawley, Neil	Bass	North Carolina School of the Arts Winston-Salem, N. C.
Brière, Andrée	Bass	Juilliard School of Music New York, N. Y.
Buchanan, Gary	Trumpet	North Carolina School of the Arts Winston-Salem, N. C.
Buckley, Richard	Trombone	North Carolina School of the Arts Winston-Salem, N. C.
Buhler, Nicolette	Flute	North Carolina School of the Arts Winston-Salem, N. C.
Byers, Harold	Violin	Juilliard School of Music New York, N. Y.
Carmitchell, Joseph	Violin	Eastman School of Music Rochester, N. Y.
Carnes, Emily	Flute	North Carolina School of the Arts Winston-Salem, N. C.
Chappell, Richard	Horn	North Carolina School of the Arts Winston-Salem, N. C.
Cordle, Andrew	Bassoon	Juilliard School of Music New York, N. Y.
Cotruvo, Arthur	Violin	Boston University Boston, Mass.
Fahrney, Edward	Trombone	—
Flax, Laura	Clarinet	Juilliard School of Music New York, N. Y.
Gardner, Ned	Trumpet	North Carolina School of the Arts Winston-Salem, N. C.
Givins, Donald	Piano	North Carolina School of the Arts Winston-Salem, N. C.
Grossman, Jerry	Cello	Curtis Institute of Music Philadelphia, Pa.
Helbein, Edward	Trumpet	Verona High School Verona, N. J.
Howard, Peter	Cello	—

Hunter, Jennifer	Harp	North Carolina School of the Arts Winston-Salem, N. C.
Ingram, Randy	Violin	Freedom High School Bethlehem, Pa.
Jacob, George	Percussion	Bergenfield High School Bergenfield, N. J.
Kotlas, Karel	Tuba	North Carolina School of the Arts Winston-Salem, N. C.
Lerew, Donna	Violin	Eastman School of Music Rochester, N. Y.
Lingelbach, Catherine	Viola	North Carolina School of the Arts Winston-Salem, N. C.
Mabry, Drake	Oboe	Manhattan School of Music New York, N. Y.
McAlhany, Nancy	Violin	Northwestern University Evanston, Ill.
Magnuson, Phil	Viola	Duke University Durham, N. C.
Manley, Todd	Percussion	North Carolina School of the Arts Winston-Salem, N. C.
Miller, Douglas	Clarinet	University of North Carolina Chapel Hill, N. C.
Moffet, Sydney	Violin	North Carolina School of the Arts Winston-Salem, N. C.
Morgan, Roger	Cello	North Carolina School of the Arts Winston-Salem, N. C.
Myers, Lucinda	Violin	University of Miami Coral Gables, Fla.
Neumann, Susan	Violin	Juilliard School of Music New York, N. Y.
Newton, John	Horn	North Carolina School of the Arts Winston-Salem, N. C.
Nield, Christine	Flute	North Carolina School of the Arts Winston-Salem, N. C.
Park, Grace	Violin	North Carolina School of the Arts Winston-Salem, N. C.
Pepe, Arlene	Piano	New England Conservatory Boston, Mass.
Plank, Steven	Trumpet	University of Louisville Louisville, Ky.
Pruett, John	Viola	North Carolina School of the Arts Winston-Salem, N. C.
Quittner, Joseph	Violin	Mannes College New York, N. Y.
Randolph, Ann	Flute	North Carolina School of the Arts Winston-Salem, N. C.
Raulston, Linda	Violin	University of Tennessee Memphis, Tenn.

Reyes-Otalora, Manuel	Violin	Columbia University New York, N. Y.
Roden, Ruth	Bassoon	North Carolina School of the Arts Winston-Salem, N. C.
Roden, Virginia	Violin	University of Northern Illinois DeKalb, Ill.
Roden, Wayne	Viola	University of Northern Illinois DeKalb, Ill.
Sanger, Sam Lloyd	Clarinet	North Carolina School of the Arts Winston-Salem, N. C.
Sarbo, Anita	Viola	Duke University Durham, N. C.
Sauvé, Robert	Viola	North Carolina School of the Arts Winston-Salem, N. C.
Scarborough, Nancy	Violin	East Carolina University Greenville, N. C.
Schiavo, Paul	Oboe	Mannes College New York, N. Y.
Siebert, Renée	Flute	North Carolina School of the Arts Winston-Salem, N. C.
Slayden, Anne	Horn	Buffalo State, Buffalo, N. Y.
Sokol, Paula	Violin	University of Washington Seattle, Wash.
Sorton, Robert	Oboe	North Carolina School of the Arts Winston-Salem, N. C.
Standaart, Peter	Flute	North Carolina School of the Arts Winston-Salem, N. C.
Stephens, Clarence	Bass	North Carolina School of the Arts Winston-Salem, N. C.
Tait, Catherine	Violin	North Carolina School of the Arts Winston-Salem, N. C.
Tait, Margaret	Cello	North Carolina School of the Arts Winston-Salem, N. C.
Wachowski, Phil	Viola	North Carolina School of the Arts Winston-Salem, N. C.
Walker, Susan	Cello	North Carolina School of the Arts Winston-Salem, N. C.
Ward, Mark	Cello	North Carolina School of the Arts Winston-Salem, N. C.
Ward, Timothy	Bassoon	North Carolina School of the Arts Winston-Salem, N. C.
Weaver, Nancy	Cello	Northwestern University Evanston, Ill.
Wholahan, John	Violin	Cornell, Ithaca, N. Y.
Williams, Delbert	Bass	Ohio State University Columbus, Ohio
Wiliams, Tommy	Percussion	North Carolina School of the Arts Winston-Salem, N. C.

1971

Aldrich, Richard	Bassoon	—
Allgeyer, Barbara	Clarinet	—
Austin, Arthur	Clarinet	Curtis Institute of Music Philadelphia, Pa.
Banks, Torrance	Trombone	University of North Carolina Chapel Hill, N. C.
Barbee, Vincent	Horn	North Carolina School of the Arts Winston-Salem, N. C.
Buckley, Richard	Trombone	North Carolina School of the Arts Winston-Salem, N. C.
Carroll, Edward	Trumpet	Interlochen Arts Academy Interlochen, Mich.
Case, Kathryn	Harp	North Carolina School of the Arts Winston-Salem, N. C.
Church, Ray	Oboe	University of North Carolina Chapel Hill, N. C.
Cooke, India	Violin	North Carolina School of the Arts Winston-Salem, N. C.
Day, Timothy	Flute	Oberlin College Oberlin, Ohio
DiPalma, Maria	Voice	Curtis Institute of Music Philadelphia, Pa.
Douvas, Elaine	Oboe	Cleveland Institute of Music Cleveland, Ohio
Endress, Mary	Voice	Interlochen Arts Academy Interlochen, Mich.
Entzi, John	Trumpet	University of North Carolina Chapel Hill, N. C.
Eringer, Sari	Viola	North Carolina School of the Arts Winston-Salem, N. C.
Evans, Anne	Violin	Emma Willard High School Troy, N. Y.
Evans, Renée	Voice	Cleveland Institute of Music Cleveland, Ohio
Fischer, Linda	Violin	North Carolina School of the Arts Winston-Salem, N. C.
Fletcher, James	Guitar	North Carolina School of the Arts Winston-Salem, N. C.
Foster, Edward	Trombone	University of Hartford Hartford, Conn.
Frey, James	Clarinet	Oberlin College Oberlin, Ohio
Friedhoff, Mark	Cello	Indiana University Bloomington, Ind.
Garrett, Margo	Piano	North Carolina School of the Arts Winston-Salem, N. C.

Genualdi, Joseph	Violin	North Carolina School of the Arts Winston-Salem, N. C.
Goldring, Michael	Bass	State University of New York Buffalo, N. Y.
Grainger, Bruce	Bassoon	Sumner High School Seattle, Wash.
Gugliotta, Ronald	Guitar	North Carolina School of the Arts Winston-Salem, N. C.
Guthrie, Robert	Guitar	North Carolina School of the Arts Winston-Salem, N. C.
Hamparian, Peter	Violin	Mannes College New York, N. Y.
Harvey, Hugh	Voice	North Carolina School of the Arts Winston-Salem, N. C.
Hawkins, Jesse	Violin	North Carolina School of the Arts Winston-Salem, N. C.
Hitchcock, Tammie	Harp	North Carolina School of the Arts Winston-Salem, N. C.
Holmes, Marymal	Voice	North Carolina School of the Arts Winston-Salem, N. C.
Hunter, Jennifer	Harp	North Carolina School of the Arts Winston-Salem, N. C.
Jezierski, Stefan	Horn	North Carolina School of the Arts Winston-Salem, N. C.
Johnson, Candace	Voice	Vassar College Poughkeepsie, N. Y.
Johnson, Scott	Trumpet	University of Wisconsin Madison, Wis.
Kahng, Wooh-Chung	Cello	Manhattan School of Music New York, N. Y.
Kautzman, Barbara	Bass	North Carolina School of the Arts Winston-Salem, N. C.
Kelly, Sherry	Voice	University of North Carolina Chapel Hill, N. C.
Koonce, Frank	Guitar	North Carolina School of the Arts Winston-Salem, N. C.
Kornblueh, Nora	Cello	Boston University Boston, Mass.
Krehbiel, James	Violin	—
Lansing, Liana	Voice	New England Conservatory Boston, Mass.
Lawrence, Ronald	Viola	Interlochen Arts Academy Interlochen, Mich.
Litvin, David	Violin	University of Michigan Ann Arbor, Mich.
Lowe, Sherman	Voice	North Carolina School of the Arts Winston-Salem, N. C.
Lynch, Dick	Violin	—

McLain, Ellen	Voice	North Carolina School of the Arts Winston-Salem, N. C.
McMillan, Claudia	Bass	North Carolina School of the Arts Winston-Salem, N. C.
Makarski, Michelle	Violin	Interlochen Arts Academy Interlochen, Mich.
Malone, Michele	Viola	Florida State University Tallahassee, Fla.
Manley, Todd	Percussion	North Carolina School of the Arts Winston-Salem, N. C.
Marvine, Jane	Oboe	Interlochen Arts Academy Interlochen, Mich.
Matson, Ralph	Violin	Oberlin College Oberlin, Ohio
Medas, Brian	Guitar	North Carolina School of the Arts Winston-Salem, N. C.
Moses, Clifford	Bass	North Carolina School of the Arts Winston-Salem, N. C.
Nagel, Alan	Bass	Interlochen Arts Academy Interlochen, Mich.
Nesper, Mark	Horn	University of Southern California Los Angeles, Calif.
Nield, Christine	Flute	North Carolina School of the Arts Winston-Salem, N. C.
Ourada, Ann	Violin	Interlochen Arts Academy Interlochen, Mich.
Parcells, Julie	Violin	North Carolina School of the Arts Winston-Salem, N. C.
Park, Grace	Violin	North Carolina School of the Arts Winston-Salem, N. C.
Patykula, John	Guitar	North Carolina School of the Arts Winston-Salem, N. C.
Perry, David	Voice	North Carolina School of the Arts Winston-Salem, N. C.
Perry, Francis	Guitar	North Carolina School of the Arts Winston-Salem, N. C.
Pittman, Nancy	Clarinet	University of North Carolina Chapel Hill, N. C.
Pope, Jerrold	Voice	Interlochen Arts Academy Interlochen, Mich.
Pruett, John	Viola	North Carolina School of the Arts Winston-Salem, N. C.
Ramp, Georgia	Violin	University of Tennessee Knoxville, Tenn.
Randolph, Laurie	Guitar	North Carolina School of the Arts Winston-Salem, N. C.
Roden, Ruth	Bassoon	North Carolina School of the Arts Winston-Salem, N. C.

Schatten, Gregory	Piano	Interlochen Arts Academy Interlochen, Mich.
Schlessinger, Mary	Guitar	North Carolina School of the Arts Winston-Salem, N. C.
Schultz, Jane	Viola	Eastman School of Music Rochester, N. Y.
Schwartz, David	Cello	Ardsley High School Ardsley, N. Y.
Shifrin, Kenneth	Trombone	Duke University Durham, N. C.
Sibley, Marjorie	Violin	Florida State University Tallahassee, Fla.
Sittenfeld, Eugene	Percussion	Eastman School of Music Rochester, N. Y.
Sittenfeld, Margorie	Flute	Eastman School of Music Rochester, N. Y.
Smith, Charlotte	Oboe	University of North Carolina Chapel Hill, N. C.
Spearman, Andrew	Horn	University of Connecticut Storrs, Conn.
Spearman, Feather	Flute	University of Connecticut Storrs, Conn.
Squires, Steven	Trumpet	—
Starks, Winifred	Harp	North Carolina School of the Arts Winston-Salem, N. C.
Stephens, Clarence	Bass	North Carolina School of the Arts Winston-Salem, N. C.
Stephenson, Donna	Voice	North Carolina School of the Arts Winston-Salem, N. C.
Stern, Paul	Guitar	Greenhill High School Dallas, Tex.
Stewart, Bradley	Violin	Juilliard School of Music New York, N. Y.
Stoughton, Michael	Cello	Juilliard School of Music New York, N. Y.
Stoughton, Renata	Piano	Oberlin School of Music Oberlin, Ohio
Thiolat, Titania	Viola	—
Thornton, Michael	Tuba	University of Cincinnati Cincinnati, Ohio
Tretick, Stephanie	Violin	Vassar College Poughkeepsie, N. Y.
Ussery, Cheryl	Horn	Manhattan School of Music New York, N. Y.
VanValkenburg, James	Viola	Interlochen Arts Academy Interlochen, Mich.
Visca, Claudia	Voice	Curtis Institute of Music Philadelphia, Pa.

Walker, Nelsie	Voice	Juilliard School of Music New York, N. Y.
Ward, Timothy	Bassoon	Curtis Institute of Music Philadelphia, Pa.
Wickham, Antonia	Cello	—
Williams, Michael	Voice	North Carolina School of the Arts Winston-Salem, N. C.
Williams, Tommy	Percussion	North Carolina School of the Arts Winston-Salem, N. C.
Wirth, Lawrence	Cello	Interlochen Arts Academy Interlochen, Mich.
Wooh, Myung Son	Cello	Manhattan School of Music New York, N. Y.

1972

Aldridge, Ben	Trumpet	Yale University New Haven, Conn.
Andrews, Marcia	Voice	Cleveland Institute of Music Cleveland, Ohio
Arnett, Roger	Guitar	University of South Carolina Columbia, S. C.
Asman, Katherine	Voice	Cleveland Institute of Music Cleveland, Ohio
Baldwin, David	Trumpet	Yale University New Haven, Conn.
Barbee, Vincent	Horn	North Carolina School of the Arts Winston-Salem, N. C.
Barnes, Catherine	Violin	Eastman School of Music Rochester, N. Y.
Becker, Jane	Flute	University of Wisconsin Madison, Wis.
Benson, Kerry	Violin	North Carolina School of the Arts Winston-Salem, N. C.
Bretschger, Fred	Bass	North Carolina School of the Arts Winston-Salem, N. C.
Brooks, Bonnie	Horn	Albany State College Albany, N. Y.
Buckley, Richard	Trombone	North Carolina School of the Arts Winston-Salem, N. C.
Buntin, Anne	Violin	—
Cafferty, Ann	Violin	Boston University Boston, Mass.
Carriker, Dianne	Voice	North Carolina School of the Arts Winston-Salem, N. C.
Casey, Amie	Violin	Walnut Hills High School Cincinnati, Ohio

Ciompi, Arturo	Clarinet	North Carolina School of the Arts Winston-Salem, N. C.
Contino, Adriana	Cello	Indiana University Bloomington, Ind.
Crowley, Robert	Clarinet	Eastman School of Music Rochester, N. Y.
Cubbage, John	Bass	Juilliard School of Music New York, N. Y.
Culbreath, Beverly	Voice	North Carolina School of the Arts Winston-Salem, N. C.
Dea, Teresa	Cello	North Carolina School of the Arts Winston-Salem, N. C.
Dodds, Joanne	Cello	University of Illinois Urbana, Ill.
Dunlap, Sam	Guitar	Mt. Desert Island High School Bar Harbour, Maine
Eckstein, Brian	Bass	New England Conservatory of Music Boston, Mass.
Egge, Marian	Violin	Eastman School of Music Rochester, N. Y.
Endress, Mary	Voice	North Carolina School of the Arts Winston-Salem, N. C.
Eringer, Sari	Violin	North Carolina School of the Arts Winston-Salem, N. C.
Felatico, Anthony	Voice	Temple University Philadelphia, Pa.
Fehling, Victoria	Cello	State University of Iowa Iowa City, Iowa
Gagliano, Dominic	Bassoon	Indiana University Bloomington, Ind.
Genualdi, Joseph	Violin	North Carolina School of the Arts Winston-Salem, N. C.
Gerald, Barbara	Violin	Texas Tech University Lubbock, Tex.
Gottlieb, Cynthia	Flute	New England Conservatory of Music Boston, Mass.
Hagnes, Helen	Violin	Juilliard School of Music New York, N. Y.
Heilbronn, Margaret	Violin	Dekalb Senior High School Atlanta, Ga.
Herrick, Elizabeth	Voice	North Carolina School of the Arts Winston-Salem, N. C.
Herskowitz, Robin	Guitar	Middlebury College Middlebury, Vt.
Hildebrant, Mary	Cello	Northwestern University Evanston, Ill.
Hoback, James	Voice	North Carolina School of the Arts Winston-Salem, N. C.

Horner, Lynn	Violin	North Carolina School of the Arts Winston-Salem, N. C.
Johnson, Dandace	Voice	Vassar College Poughkeepsie, N. Y.
Johnson, Scott	Flute	Wesleyan University Middletown, Conn.
Kay, Nancy	Harp	Villa Schifanoia, Florence
Kenny, Gayle	Bass	Duke University, Durham, N. C.
Kimenker, Nina	Cello	Boston University Boston, Mass.
Kolmas, Hilary	Violin	University of Illinois Urbana, Ill.
Kuentzel, Craig	Trumpet	North Carolina School of the Arts Winston-Salem, N. C.
Lane, Stephen	Cello	Chesterton High School Chesterton, Ind.
Lee, Hitai	Violin	North Carolina School of the Arts Winston-Salem, N. C.
Longmire, David	Bassoon	Yale University New Haven, Conn.
Lowe, Sherman	Voice	North Carolina School of the Arts Winston-Salem, N. C.
Manley, Todd	Percussion	North Carolina School of the Arts Winston-Salem, N. C.
Medas, Brian	Guitar	North Carolina School of the Arts Winston-Salem, N. C.
Pancarowicz, Raymond	Violin	Eastman School of Music Rochester, N. Y.
Parcells, Julie	Violin	North Carolina School of the Arts Winston-Salem, N. C.
Parsons, Steve	Percussion	University of Miami Coral Gables, Fla.
Patykula, John	Guitar	North Carolina School of the Arts Winston-Salem, N. C.
Perry, Francis	Guitar	North Carolina School of the Arts Winston-Salem, N. C.
Pors, Christiane	Violin	North Carolina School of the Arts Winston-Salem, N. C.
Pretat, Richard	Bass	Oberlin College Oberlin, Ohio
Proctor, Margaret	Violin	University of North Carolina Chapel Hill, N. C.
Radin, Beverly	Flute	Manhattan School of Music New York, N. Y.
Randolph, Laurie	Guitar	Peabody Conservatory Baltimore, Md.
Raphals, Philip	Cello	Yale University New Haven, Conn.

Reasoner, Barry	Trombone	Ball State University Muncie, Ind.
Robbins, Marilyn	Voice	North Carolina School of the Arts Winston-Salem, N. C.
Rudkin, Ronald	Clarinet	East Carolina University Greenville, N. C.
Rustman, Mark	Oboe	Juilliard School of Music New York, N. Y.
Schmidt, Kimberly	Piano	Eastman School of Music Rochester, N. Y.
Shapiro, Madeleine	Cello	Manhattan School of Music New York, N. Y.
Shiff, Mikki	Voice	University of Miami Coral Gables, Fla.
Shipps, Stephen	Violin	Indiana University, Bloomington, Ind.
Sills, Barry	Cello	Eastern Hills High School Fort Worth, Tex.
Smith, Debbie	Voice	North Carolina School of the Arts Winston-Salem, N. C.
Smith, Valerian	Cello	North Carolina School of the Arts Winston-Salem, N. C.
Solomon, Gerald	Percussion	North Carolina School of the Arts Winston-Salem, N. C.
Sorce, Mary Ellen	Viola	Albany State College Albany, N. Y.
Soren, Mary	Viola	Rhode Island College Providence, R. I.
Stadler, Mark	Guitar	North Carolina School of the Arts Winston-Salem, N. C.
Starker, Gwen	Violin	Indiana University Bloomington, Ind.
Stenger, Gordon	Oboe	University of Michigan Ann Arbor, Mich.
Stephen, Arecia	Viola	University of Michigan Ann Arbor, Mich.
Stephenson, Donna	Voice	East Carolina University Greenville, N. C.
Sublette, Mary	Viola	Portales High School Portales, N. Mex.
Thornton, Michael	Tuba	University of Cincinnati Cincinnati, Ohio
Trapassi, Barbara	Violin	—
Turner, William	Voice	North Carolina School of the Arts Winston-Salem, N. C.
Van Derven, Herbert	Trombone	New England Conservatory of Music Boston, Mass.
Van Valkenburg, James	Viola	University of Indiana Bloomington, Ind.

Wachowski, Phil	Viola	North Carolina School of the Arts Winston-Salem, N. C.
Wade, Irene	Viola	North Carolina School of the Arts Winston-Salem, N. C.
Waite, Louise	Oboe	Hartt College Philadelphia, Pa.
Waite, Norman	Horn	Yale University New Haven, Conn.
Ward, Timothy	Bassoon	Curtis Institute of Music Philadelphia, Pa.
Weist, Anhared	Violin	Hartt College Philadelphia, Pa.
White, Carolyn	Bass	Indiana University Bloomington, Ind.
Whitener, Carolyn	Horn	Ohio University Athens, Ohio
Williams, Susan	Cello	University of Illinois Urbana, Ill.
Wood, David	Guitar	University of North Carolina Chapel Hill, N. C.